THE CAMBRIDGE BIBLE COMMENTARY

NEW ENGLISH BIBLE

GENERAL EDITORS
P. R. ACKROYD, A. R. C. LEANEY
J. W. PACKER

ISAIAH 40–66

THE BOOK OF THE PROPHET
ISAIAH

CHAPTERS 40–66

COMMENTARY BY
A. S. HERBERT

*Professor Emeritus of Old Testament Studies in the
Selly Oak Colleges, Birmingham*

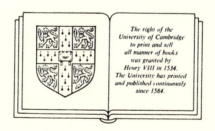

The right of the
University of Cambridge
to print and sell
all manner of books
was granted by
Henry VIII in 1534.
The University has printed
and published continuously
since 1584.

CAMBRIDGE UNIVERSITY PRESS

CAMBRIDGE

LONDON   NEW YORK   NEW ROCHELLE
MELBOURNE   SYDNEY

CAMBRIDGE UNIVERSITY PRESS
Cambridge, New York, Melbourne, Madrid, Cape Town, Singapore, São Paulo

Cambridge University Press
The Edinburgh Building, Cambridge CB2 8RU, UK

Published in the United States of America by Cambridge University Press, New York

www.cambridge.org
Information on this title: www.cambridge.org/9780521207218

First published 1975
Reprinted 1980, 1986
Re-issued in this digitally printed version 2008

A catalogue record for this publication is available from the British Library

Library of Congress Cataloguing in Publication data

Bible. O.T. Isaiah 40–66. English. New English.
The book of the Propet Isaiah, Chapters 40–66.

(The Cambridge Bible commentary, New English Bible)
Includes index.
1. Bible. O.T. Isaiah 40–66–Commentaries.
I. Hebert, Arthur Sumner. II. Title. III. Series

BS 1520. H47 1975   224′.1   74-16997

ISBN 978-0-521-20721-8 hardback
ISBN 978-0-521-09933-2 paperback

GENERAL EDITORS' PREFACE

The aim of this series is to provide the text of the New English Bible closely linked to a commentary in which the results of modern scholarship are made available to the general reader. Teachers and young people have been especially kept in mind. The commentators have been asked to assume no specialized theological knowledge, and no knowledge of Greek and Hebrew. Bare references to other literature and multiple referencss to other parts of the Bible have been avoided. Actual quotations have been given as often as possible.

The completion of the New Testament series in 1967 provided a basis for the production of the much larger Old Testament and Apocrypha series, which was completed in 1979. The welcome accorded to the earlier volumes encouraged the editors to follow the same general pattern, and an attempt was made to take account of criticisms which had been offered. One necessary change has been the inclusion of the translators' footnotes, since in the Old Testament these are more extensive, and essential for the understanding of the text.

Within the severe limits imposed by the size and scope of the series, each commentator has attempted to set out the main findings of recent biblical scholarship and to describe the historical background of the text. The main theological issues have also been critically discussed.

Much attention has been given to the form of the volumes. The aim is to produce books each of which will be read consecutively from first to last page. The introductory material leads naturally into the text, which itself leads into the alternating sections of the commentary.

The series is accompanied by three volumes of a more general character. *Understanding the Old Testament* sets out to provide the larger historical and archaeological background, to say something about the life and thought of the people of the Old Testament, and to answer the question 'Why should we study the Old Testament?'. *The Making of the Old Testament* is concerned with the formation of the books of the Old Testament and Apocrypha in the context of the ancient near eastern world, and with the ways in which these books have come down to us in the life of the Jewish and Christian communities. *Old Testament Illustrations* contains maps, diagrams and photographs with an explanatory text. These three volumes are designed to provide material helpful to the understanding of the individual books and their commentaries, but they are also prepared so as to be of use quite independently.

P. R. A.
A. R. C. L.
J. W. P.

CONTENTS

THE FOOTNOTES TO THE
N.E.B. TEXT

The footnotes to the N.E.B. text are designed to help the reader either to understand particular points of detail – the meaning of a name, the presence of a play upon words – or to give information about the actual text. Where the Hebrew text appears to be erroneous, or there is doubt about its precise meaning, it may be necessary to turn to manuscripts which offer a different wording, or to ancient translations of the text which may suggest a better reading, or to offer a new explanation based upon conjecture. In such cases, the footnotes supply very briefly an indication of the evidence, and whether the solution proposed is one that is regarded as possible or as probable. Various abbreviations are used in the footnotes.

(1) Some abbreviations are simply of terms used in explaining a point: *ch(s).*, chapter(s); *cp.*, compare; *lit.*, literally; *mng.*, meaning; *MS(S).*, manuscript(s), i.e. Hebrew manuscript(s), unless otherwise stated; *om.*, omit(s); *or*, indicating an alternative interpretation; *poss.*, possible; *prob.*, probable; *rdg.*, reading; *Vs(s).*, Version(s).

(2) Other abbreviations indicate sources of information from which better interpretations or readings may be obtained.

Aq. Aquila, a Greek translator of the Old Testament (perhaps about A.D. 130) characterized by great literalness.

Aram. Aramaic – may refer to the text in this language (used in parts of Ezra and Daniel), or to the meaning of an Aramaic word. Aramaic belongs to the same language family as Hebrew, and is known from about 1000 B.C. over a wide area of the Middle East, including Palestine.

Heb. Hebrew – may refer to the Hebrew text or may indicate the literal meaning of the Hebrew word.

Josephus Flavius Josephus (A.D. 37/8–about 100), author of the *Jewish Antiquities*, a survey of the whole history of his people, directed partly at least to a non-Jewish audience, and of various other works, notably one on the *Jewish War* (that of A.D. 66–73) and a defence of Judaism (*Against Apion*).

Luc. Sept. Lucian's recension of the Septuagint, an important edition made in Antioch in Syria about the end of the third century A.D.

Pesh. Peshitta or Peshitto, the Syriac version of the Old Testament. Syriac is the name given chiefly to a form of Eastern Aramaic used by the Christian community. The translation varies in quality, and is at many points influenced by the Septuagint or the Targums.

Sam. Samaritan Pentateuch – the form of the first five books of the Old Testament as used by the Samaritan community. It is written in Hebrew in a special form of the Old Hebrew script, and preserves an important form of the text, somewhat influenced by Samaritan ideas.

Scroll(s) Scroll(s), commonly called the Dead Sea Scrolls, found at or near Qumran from 1947 onwards. These important manuscripts shed light on the state of the Hebrew text as it was developing in the last centuries B.C. and the first century A.D.

Sept. Septuagint (meaning 'seventy'; often abbreviated as the Roman numeral LXX), the name given to the main Greek version of the Old Testament. According to tradition, the Pentateuch was translated in Egypt in the third century B.C. by 70 (or 72) translators, six from each tribe, but the precise nature of its origin and development is not fully known. It was intended to provide Greek-speaking Jews with a convenient translation. Subsequently it came to be much revered by the Christian community.

Symm. Symmachus, another Greek translator of the Old Testament (beginning of the third century A.D.), who tried to combine literalness with good style. Both Lucian and Jerome viewed his version with favour.

Targ. Targum, a name given to various Aramaic versions of the Old Testament, produced over a long period and eventually standardized, for the use of Aramaic-speaking Jews.

Theod. Theodotion, the author of a revision of the Septuagint (probably second century A.D.) very dependent on the Hebrew text.

Vulg. Vulgate, the most important Latin version of the Old Testament, produced by Jerome about A.D. 400, and the text most used throughout the Middle Ages in western Christianity.

[. . .] In the text itself square brackets are used to indicate probably late additions to the Hebrew text.

(Fuller discussion of a number of these points may be found in *The Making of the Old Testament* in this series)

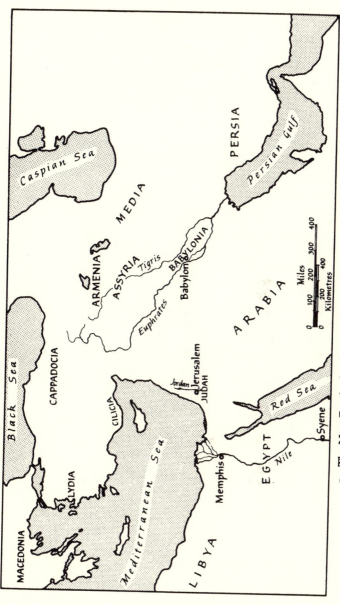

1 The Near East in the time of the Neo-Babylonian and Persian Empires

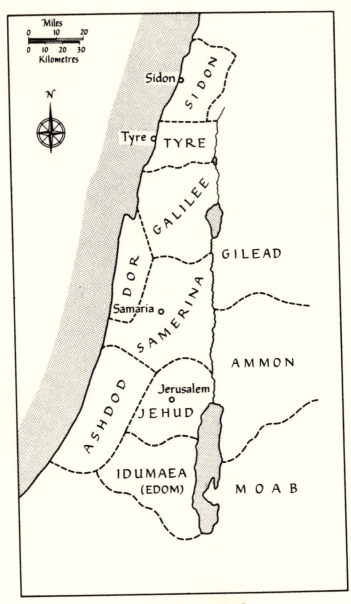

2 Judah under Persian rule

THE BOOK OF THE PROPHET

ISAIAH

✡ ✡ ✡ ✡ ✡ ✡ ✡ ✡ ✡ ✡ ✡ ✡ ✡ ✡

THE RENEWAL OF ISRAEL

The whole sixty-six chapters of the book of Isaiah were written on one scroll. This is what appears from the New Testament references (e.g. Matt. 12: 17–21), is demonstrated by the Dead Sea Scroll of Isaiah (first century B.C.) and is assumed by Ecclus. 48: 24–5 (about 180 B.C.). It is true that none of these was arguing for, or seeking to establish, questions of authorship, but they point to the fact that our book of Isaiah existed in this form by 200 B.C. The book itself is divided into two unequal sections by chs. 36–9, a historical excerpt taken from the book of Kings (2 Kings 18: 13 – 20: 19) describing the tragic events that occurred in and around Jerusalem at the close of Isaiah's ministry. This excerpt was apparently chosen with some care, since it ends (39: 6–7) with a warning of the fate that will befall the descendants of Hezekiah at the hands of the Babylonians. This is the situation to which Isa. 40 addresses itself, and this continues throughout the following chapters. The world power is no longer Assyria, as it was in the eighth century B.C. but Babylon, or to be more precise, Babylon about to fall to the Persian King Cyrus. The impending collapse of the Babylonian Empire (47: 1–15) and the victorious career of Cyrus (44: 28 – 45: 7) are specifically mentioned. They are described as the work of God for the release and restoration of his people who have been exiled from their land (43: 5–7; 48: 20), and for the rebuilding of Zion (52: 1–2; 54: 11–13). Those who are addressed will be the witnesses that he who is bringing these events to pass is the

LORD, the Holy One of Israel (43: 10–15). Chs. 40–66 belong, then, to a period from about 547 B.C. when the Babylonian power was weakening before the might of Cyrus and the rise of the Medo-Persian Empire. We may note that Isa. 34–5 also reflects the circumstances of the Babylonian exile and has points of resemblance to Isa. 40–66.

There is, however, a noticeable difference between Isa. 40–55 and Isa. 56–66. The scene in which chs. 56–66 are set is not Babylon but Palestine, or more precisely Jerusalem and the district round about. Some exiles have returned, though to conditions very different from those promised in chs. 40–55; the temple has been rebuilt and the sacrificial system restored (56: 7; 60: 7). Yet a spirit of disillusionment has grown, since the physical conditions of life are very different from those suggested in Isa. 40–55, and there has developed a breakdown of social justice (56: 9 – 57: 1) which recalls the kind of problems so often reflected in prophecy before the exile, as for example Isa. 5: 20–3. Allusions to known historical events are too few and uncertain to allow for a definite conclusion, but an approximate date would be around 500 B.C., after Zechariah and before Nehemiah.

Whether we have the words of one prophet or more than one is again a matter of dispute. It is hardly probable that the prophet of Isa. 63: 1–6 can be identified with the author of the Servant Poems (cp. p. 9), or, for that matter, 66: 18–24. The simplest solution is to see chs. 56–66 as coming from that continuing community of Isaiah's disciples whose faith was kindled and invigorated by the words of Isa. 40–55.

Isa. 40–55 may be regarded as substantially the work of one prophet. Questions have been raised about the authorship of four poems (42: 1–4; 49: 1–6; 50: 4–9; 52: 13 – 53: 12) and these are discussed separately (pp. 9–14). The difficulty of accounting for their separation from one another, their inclusion at points where at least they are appropriate to the context, and the general similarity of literary style, allow us to

2

regard them as the work of the same prophet–poet as the rest of chs. 40–55.

Although the main thought is the same throughout, there is a recognizable division within these chapters which seems to suggest a change in the historical situation. The division would come at Isa. 48. Thus, in chs. 40–8 Cyrus and Babylon are named; they do not appear in chs. 49–55. Also lacking in the closing chapters are the contemptuous references to idol-gods. While in chs. 40–8 those addressed are usually Jacob–Israel, in chs. 49–55 they are Zion–Jerusalem. A reasonable explanation would be to see Isa. 40–8 as leading up to the surrender of Babylon to Cyrus in 538 B.C. while chs. 49–55 are concerned to prepare the exiles for their return to Palestine, and the fulfilment of their ancient role in the divine purpose. For the sake of convenience we may speak of the prophet of Isa. 40–55 as Second Isaiah, and use the term Third Isaiah for the prophet or prophets of Isa. 56–66. We use these terms because we do not know the names of the prophets whose oracles occur in these chapters.

The chronological distinction between Isa. 40–66 and Isa. 1–39 is accompanied by a difference of style and vocabulary, and also a difference of theological interest, the latter being made necessary by the totally new circumstances of those addressed (see pp. 4–7). The style of Isa. 40–66 is distinctive and will be readily apparent to those who read aloud from these chapters. It is marked by a lyrical quality, and this in itself presents a difficulty for the translator. It is always difficult to translate the poetry of one language into another. While most prophets uttered their oracles in poetic form, those oracles were brief, not usually more than two or three verses. In Isa. 40–66, however, there is a greater degree of sustained poetry, e.g. Isa. 42: 10–17, 18–25, often expressed in a hymn resembling such Psalms as 96, 97 and 98. Together with the hymns we find a variety of forms: exhortation (51: 1–8), legal argument as though in a law court (41: 21–9), a taunt song (47). A liturgical pattern may be recognized in 63: 7 – 65: 19

3

in which penitential prayer, supplication and a divine answer can be heard. The passage 59: 9–15 is a prayer of confession following the reproach of 59: 1–8. The great statement of 56: 1–8 which introduces the closing section of this part of the book might be heard as the law of the Kingdom of God for the returned exiles.

It has been suggested that much of Second Isaiah had already appeared in written form before the time of final compilation, whether by the prophet himself or his disciples. Undoubtedly these chapters show evidence of deliberate compilation, reaching a climax in chs. 54 and 55. We shall notice frequent allusions to Israel's psalms and this may well suggest that the various sections were first addressed to a worshipping congregation in which the prophet was a prominent figure. This is prophecy of which the forms of expression are conditioned by the hymns and prayers of Israel's worship. In view of his great importance in the life of the later Jewish community and the Christian Church, we may regret that so little can be inferred about the prophet as an individual. But just as an artist never puts his name to the ikon he has painted, because for him and the worshippers that is unimportant, so what really mattered was the word of the LORD which the prophet uttered and his disciples gratefully received; his name was lost in the splendour of his message. Perhaps it is not surprising that the words for praise, glory and joy occur so frequently in these chapters. There could have been little in the conditions under which the exiles lived to justify such language, but this prophet had seen the glory of the LORD, Creator of the world and Ruler of history.

THE HISTORICAL BACKGROUND

The text of Second Isaiah makes quite clear that these prophecies were addressed to exiles in Babylon (48: 20). Other passages referring to Babylon are only appropriate to that empire (e.g. the gods of Babylon in 46: 1, 2). From 2 Kings

Table of events relating to Isaiah 40–66

The Jewish People	Literature	Neo-Babylonian Empire
Jehoiakim 609–598	Jeremiah 626–580	Nebuchadrezzar II 605–562
Jehoiachin 598–597 first capture of Jerusalem; some Jews deported 597		
Zedekiah 597–587/586 fall of Jerusalem destruction of temple second deportation 587/586	Ezekiel 593–571	
third deportation 581	Lamentations (about 580–540)	Amel Marduk 562–560
		Neriglissar 560–556
	Isaiah 40–55 (about 540)	Nabonidus 556–539
first return from Babylon 537		**Persian Empire** Cyrus 550–530
temple rebuilt 520–516/515	Haggai 520 Zechariah 520–516/515 Isaiah 55–66 (about 500) Obadiah Malachi ?450	Cambyses 530–522 Darius I 522–486 Xerxes I 486–465 Artaxerxes I 465–423

24 and 25 we learn of the Babylonian invasion of Judah, the destruction of the temple in Jerusalem and the deportation of some thousands of the population to Babylonia. There are more references in Jeremiah and Ezekiel. Further evidence of the same historical situation may be found in the descriptions of the desolated land of Judah and the ruined temple (Isa. 44: 26–8; 58: 12). Perhaps the most striking evidence is the

explicit reference to the chief human agent in the downfall of the Babylonian Empire, by name, Cyrus. In 44: 28 – 45: 4 we are told that he had been chosen by God to release God's people and restore the Holy Land.

At the beginning of the exile period the despair and hope-lessness of the Jews had been lifted by the appearance of the prophet Ezekiel. Although few paid heed to his words, yet he was, as a prophet, clear evidence of Yahweh's presence; and part of his message was of a mighty act of restoration. But the years passed and there was no release. Most of the first-generation exiles had died and a new generation had grown up with no first-hand knowledge of Palestine, Jerusalem, or the worship of the temple. Although they retained many of their ancient customs and religious practices, they were becoming rooted in the land to which they had been taken. We may imagine the seduction of the magnificent temples, the ceremonial of Babylonian religion, and all the evidence of power associated with Babylonian life and culture. It is no wonder that they began to think there was no future for the Jews as a people of Yahweh. Either the gods of Babylon had proved stronger than Yahweh, or Yahweh had abandoned them. But events were shaping (or, as the prophet would see it, 'God was shaping events') otherwise. A neighbouring people to the Babylonians, the Medes, held in vassallage the state of Anshan. The ruler of Anshan was Cyrus. He led a revolt against his overlord, Astyages, the king of Media. In this he was supported by the king of Babylon, Nabonidus, who probably thought the revolt would be to his advantage since the Median Empire was a potential rival to Babylon. This was an action he was to regret, for Cyrus soon replaced Astyages as ruler of Media. He then proceeded to extend Median sovereignty over Lydia and Cilicia in Asia Minor, and conducted successful campaigns in the east towards India. This meant that Babylonia was confronted by a vigorous empire extending from the Persian Gulf to the coast of the Mediterranean. At the same time there was growing unrest in

Babylon against Nabonidus. For reasons that are not clear he spent a considerable time in Teima in North Arabia, an important trade-centre, and left the control of Babylon to his son Bel-shar-usur (Belshazzar in Dan. 5: 1), and his neglect of the great religious festivals in Babylon, especially the New Year Festival, gained him the hostility of the priests. In 539/538 after a pitched battle at Opis on the banks of the Tigris, Cyrus was able to capture Babylon itself without a blow. He was even welcomed as a liberator. The Persian Empire had come into being, an empire greater than any that had existed before. Cyrus was more than a military genius. He created an administrative system which, with minor modifications, was to last for the next 200 years. He was extraordinarily tolerant of the customs and religions of his conquered peoples. He allowed the captives to return to their native land, taking with them their religious objects. Some Jews did so in 538 B.C. and others followed later. The temple was rebuilt by 516, and the worship of God was restored to its ancient site in the reign of Darius (522–486 B.C.).

Historically it was a period in which one great empire fell before another. Various causes may be adduced for this mighty reversal of the Babylonian Empire – political, social and economic. They can be inferred from contemporary documents and traditions. But the Hebrew prophet not only saw the events in terms of the will of God, he asserted that God was in fact directly acting in these events, that he raised up Cyrus, assured him of victory, had in fact designated him for this very purpose in order that Yahweh's people might be released from exile to take up again their strange mission of manifesting the will of God to the pagan world. They had miserably failed in the past and had reaped the fruits of failure. But God's purpose was still to be fulfilled through Israel. It was not for Israel's glorification that God was so acting but 'For my honour, for my own honour I did it' (48: 11).

THE MESSAGE OF SECOND ISAIAH

The clue to understanding this prophet's message may be found in the words 'good news'; it is obviously the gospel of the glory of God. It is a message that could only have been proclaimed by one who was wholly devoted to Israel's God, and wholly devoted to Israel as the people of God. He was a prophet, in succession to the prophets who went before him, but the message he gave also points forward to a new way of life for his people. It is small wonder that it was understood by the New Testament writers as a foretelling of the one who, they claimed, brought this prophet's good news to fulfilment in a life. His message was such as to compel expression in lyrical poetry. 'Sing' is a word that occurs more frequently in these chapters than in any other prophetic book. If we recognize, as we must, a depth of theological insight in these chapters, the prophet's creed is one to be sung rather than recited. Only a poet could and can do justice to his thought. Throughout these chapters there are references to the ancient faith of Israel; his gospel is still what Israel had already accepted. Yet the unprecedented circumstances in which that gospel was proclaimed demanded new understanding and expression of the faith once and for all received. Prophets before him saw that the events of their day were leading to the goal of the divine purpose. The book of Ezekiel expresses the same confidence about this as it prepares the people for life and worship in the New Age in which the supreme reality would be seen in the renaming of Jerusalem as 'The LORD is there' (Ezek. 48: 35, N.E.B. footnote). For Second Isaiah the hopes of earlier prophets, and expectations implicit in many of the psalms, were on the threshold of experience. It was his task to declare that the kingly rule of God was at hand; to say this to these humiliated exiles who might well be excused for finding it incredible. He must declare this in terms of their present situation and also prepare them for the role they must exercise in the New Age. What is about to happen is the work of God, and of him alone. Yet if his Glory is to be seen and known by all mankind, and by Israel in particular, then Israel must respond in trust and obedience, to enter the Kingdom. If in these chapters his language appears to us (as it must have done to his hearers) fantastic hyperbole, we must recognize that he is seeking to communicate to them his own unshakable certainty. The fact that in the short term he failed and that the events that followed after 538 B.C. fell immeasurably below his glowing expectations is frankly recognized in Isa. 56–66 as well as in prophets after the exile, Haggai, Zechariah, Malachi. Yet his words were preserved and used during the years that followed, most notably by the early Christian community as loyal men and women hesitantly entered the Kingdom, and reaffirmed the message of the prophet.

THE SERVANT POEMS

The poems are to be found at 42: 1–4; 49: 1–6; 50: 4–9; 52: 13 – 53: 12. From time to time additional verses have been associated with the first three poems, and some would add 61: 1–3 (or even the whole chapter). This delimitation (which was first suggested by B. Duhm in 1892) is generally accepted. The poems are conventionally called 'Servant Songs'. 'Songs' is not very appropriate since there is no evidence that they were intended to be sung. They are poems of a quite distinctive character. The portrayal of the Servant and his function in the purpose of God has prompted a number of questions. The two main questions before us are –

  1. Is the author of the poems the same as the author of Isa. 40–55?

  2. Of whom does the prophet speak, of himself or another?

1. *Authorship*

On literary grounds there is no good reason for distinguishing the author of these poems from the author of the rest of Isa. 40–55, but consideration of the Servant in the poems and elsewhere does raise the question whether the same prophet could be responsible for both portraits. In the sections other than the poems he is despondent, sinful, suffering indeed, but for his own sins, and humiliated by his enemies. But being redeemed by God he is a witness to mankind of God's power and forgiving love. In the poems the Servant is trustful and obedient, suffering not for his own sins, but at the hand of God for the sins of others. He intercedes and becomes God's agent for the world's salvation, courageously engages in this task, and mysteriously effects God's saving purpose through suffering and death. In the sections other than the poems the Servant is identified with Israel. In the poems this is not so except at 49: 3 ('my servant, Israel') which is followed by a statement that the Servant has a mission to Israel which is then extended to 'earth's farthest bounds'.

Who then was the author of the poems? At first sight, the simplest explanation would seem to be that these poems were by another author. A collection of prophetic oracles might well include sayings by more than one prophet, as may be seen in Isa. 1–39. Yet this suggestion creates its own problems. There is an obvious development of thought as we move from one poem to another, reaching a climax in the fourth poem. Whoever was responsible for the present literary form of Isa. 40–55 seems to have worked with a clear plan, conscious of chronology in recording the oracles and continuity of thought leading to a dramatic climax in ch. 55. Why then were the poems separated and placed in their present contexts?

2. *Who is the Servant?*

The attempts to answer this question have been so many and varied, presented with such persuasive arguments, that it would be arrogant to claim finality for any solution. It is easier to find objections to any answer, than to offer one that is adequate.

Some of the most sensitive Jewish thinkers have seen the Servant as Israel, so often persecuted through the centuries after the exile. Christian interpreters from New Testament days onwards, and apparently Jesus himself, have understood the prophet, especially in Isa. 53, as pointing to Christ. These interpretations may be regarded as fulfilments of prophecy rather than an answer to the question 'What did the prophet mean in his own day as he spoke to the people before him?' It is reasonable to assume that the prophet was speaking to a people in need of a word of the LORD in their situation, and that they would understand him even if they did not accept his word. It is a prophetic word requiring trust and obedience, a loyal and immediate response. It might not be accepted but it would have to be intelligible. When we ask 'Who is the Servant?' we are really trying to take our place with those who, as exiles in Babylon, heard the words of the prophet.

The emphasis in these poems is not so much on the identity of the Servant as on his function in the divine purpose.

Would they have thought of some individual in their history? Certainly the description of the Servant suggests someone like Jeremiah, yet such identification is hardly suitable for the universal mission required of the Servant, still less for the effect of his work as seen in the fourth poem. Was the prophet referring to someone in their midst? Such an individual is unknown to us and has disappeared from the pages of history, unless it be the prophet himself. But this would require another author for Isa. 53 where the Servant appears to have been put to death, and to have aroused the attention of kings and nations, who seem to have been unaffected by this prophet. This, however, is a prosaic interpretation of what is essentially great poetry and does not do justice to the biblical use of 'death' (cp. 53: 7–9).

Was he referring to one who was yet to come – a king of the Davidic line (The Lord's Anointed)? But the promise of a future king would hardly create hope in the minds of his hearers. Although the coronation hymns, e.g. Pss. 2 and 72, speak of a world-wide dominion, there is no suggestion of world-wide salvation effected through suffering. Even if there had been a ritual of humiliation for the king in the monarchical period, and this remains hypothetical for Israel's cultus, the language of the third and fourth poems seems too exaggerated for such a ritual act.

Yet in the portrait that the prophet draws it is impossible not to recognize that he is speaking of a real person, so real that we see features appropriate to a prophet or a king or even a priest. Here is one who is called by God, given a message, equipped for his task, and sustained when rejected by those he must serve. Finally his self-abandonment to the divine purpose brings him to suffering unto death which he willingly accepts as the means by which the divine energies towards reconciliation are released for sinful men. The suffering imposed becomes the suffering accepted.

The rejection of the Servant is seen as the rejection of the Servant's Lord. The nations, at last quickened to repentance, are restored to God through the self-offering of the Servant; God vindicates his faithful servant, and by his self-identification with the sinful nations he becomes the channel whereby the royal and priestly blessing penetrates their life.

All this is presented in personal, not abstract, terms; as concrete reality, not theory nor as an ideal. Can any individual known to the prophet or his hearers be seen as adequate to the task?

A person is not necessarily an individual; he can be a community. Frequently a social group is spoken of in individual terms. Thus in 1 Sam. 5: 10f. the plural pronouns in N.E.B. are singular in the Hebrew: 'me, my'. In Deut. 4–9 Israel is addressed as a single person, the commands being in the second person singular (cp. the Authorized Version and the Revised Version). Isaiah describes the nation as a severely wounded individual (Isa. 1: 5–6). Throughout Isa. 40–55 when God is described as 'Holy One', 'Maker', 'Ransomer', 'Saviour of Israel', the pronouns referring to Israel are singular (N.E.B. 'you, your'; Authorized Version and Revised Version 'thee, thy'). Similarly Israel is described as the LORD's servant. In these Servant Poems, therefore, the hearers would naturally equate the Servant with Israel. How would they understand the difference in portrayal and function? How can blind and deaf Israel also be receptive, or the despondent be courageous, or the sinful be the sinless sufferer and intercessor? We may understand the prophet as speaking to his people, knowing their failure, rebelliousness and unworthiness, for which they have suffered. They have not been abandoned by God, but in fact have been 'ransomed, healed, restored, forgiven' and so reborn to take up what was from the beginning their ancient role. He is not speaking to some ideal community, and not necessarily the 'righteous remnant'. It is the actual Israel in the moment of redemption, whose restoration to Palestine is a restoration to its true place in the purpose of God, to be, although the phrase is not specifically used by the prophet, a 'kingdom of priests' (Exod. 19: 6). We may recall that the Rabbis of the first century A.D. with a full knowledge of Israel's past and present unworthiness can understand Israel as God's bride, and so interpreted the Song of Songs. Similarly Paul, with no illusions about the Christian community, speaks of the Church as Christ's body.

We are still left with the difficulty in Isa. 49: 1–6 in which the Servant is first identified with Israel (verse 3) and then described as having a mission to restore Israel (verse 5) which is then transcended to become a mission to the nations, 'to earth's farthest bounds' (verse 6). While there are problems in the translation of the poem, we may accept the N.E.B., which presents the difficulties of interpretation clearly. If the Servant is Israel, how can Israel have a mission to Israel? Here we must recall that Israel is not only Israel in the present, but continuous with, and inclusive of, Israel of the past and in the future. The poem may be understood as saying that Israel, now redeemed, is the means whereby faithless Israel in its long history is to be restored, and so enabled to recognize its true destiny in relation to the world of mankind. The past, for the prophet, is never dead and done with. It can be redeemed and indeed must be if God be truly the God of history. The Israel of the past lives on in the Israel of the present and must share in the experience of the present. This is what the Old Testament is all about. Israel's history is, at one level, a record of failure which must be God's failure as well as man's, since God has involved himself in the life of the people. Yet it is also a record of triumph since, especially through the prophets and in Israel's great acts of worship, Israel is recalled and penitently responds to its function in the world's salvation. Israel, with all its contradictions, in its past, present and future is one, and never more truly so than in the thought of this prophet. Such an approach to these poems and to their whole context suggests that we must beware of making an artificial separation between different parts of the material in these chapters. The message of the prophet is one in all its richness.

It may be seen that the great Jewish interpreters of the Middle Ages were justified in understanding the Servant, especially as he is described in Isa. 53, as the Jewish community so often suffering persecution yet so often contributing to the world's knowledge of God. The Christian, too, is justified in seeing the poems fulfilled in Jesus Christ, if they see him as gathering into himself the life of that people in whose midst he was born, to whom he had a mission which could only be realized as that mission reached out 'to the ends of the earth'. Finally, continuing the prophet's use of the 'Servant of the LORD' for Israel, we may see the Servant as that Community which, according to Paul, is 'in Christ'; cp. 1 Cor. 1: 30; Phil. 1: 1.

✳ ✳ ✳ ✳ ✳ ✳ ✳ ✳ ✳ ✳ ✳ ✳ ✳ ✳

News of the returning exiles

GOOD NEWS FOR ZION

Comfort, comfort my people;[a]   **40**
 – it is the voice of your God;
speak tenderly to Jerusalem[b]   2
  and tell her this,
that she has fulfilled her term of bondage,
  that her penalty is paid;
she has received at the LORD's hand
  double[c] measure for all her sins.

There is a voice that cries:
Prepare a road for the LORD through the   3
  wilderness,
clear a highway across the desert for our God.
  Every valley shall be lifted up,
every mountain and hill brought down;   4
rugged places shall be made smooth
  and mountain-ranges become a plain.
Thus shall the glory of the LORD be revealed,
and all mankind together shall see it;   5
  for the LORD himself has spoken.

A voice says, 'Cry',
and another asks,[d] 'What shall I cry?'   6
'That all mankind is grass,
they last no longer than a flower of the field.

[a] Comfort...people: *or* Comfort, O my people, comfort.
[b] speak...Jerusalem: *or* bid Jerusalem be of good heart.
[c] double: *or* full.   [d] *Or, with Scroll,* and I asked.

15

7   The grass withers, the flower fades,
        when the breath of[a] the LORD blows upon them;[b]
8   the grass withers, the flowers fade,
        but the word of our God endures for evermore.'

9   You who bring Zion good news,[c] up with you to
            the mountain-top;
        lift up your voice and shout,
        you who bring good news to Jerusalem,[d]
            lift it up fearlessly;
        cry to the cities of Judah, 'Your God is here.'
10   Here is the Lord GOD coming in might,
        coming to rule with his right arm.
            His recompense comes with him,
            he carries his reward before him.
11   He will tend his flock like a shepherd
        and gather them together with his arm;
        he will carry the lambs in his bosom
            and lead the ewes to water.

✵ These verses are a prologue to chs. 40–55, of which 55:
5–13 may be read as an epilogue.

The format of the N.E.B. suggests that we have here four
brief poems or parts of one poem, and together these represent the call of the prophet to his mission. He is to announce
the promise of salvation. The exiles have suffered long but
need to recognize this as part of God's purpose. The exile was
a consequence of their refusal to recognize the LORD. A people
who had found 'no one to bring her comfort' (Lam. 1: 2–9)

[a] the breath of: *or* a wind from.
[b] *Prob. rdg.; Heb. adds* surely the people are grass.
[c] You...news: *or* O Zion, bringer of good news.
[d] you...Jerusalem: *or* O Jerusalem, bringer of good news.

will now be freed from their distress. The divine word rings throughout the heavenly courts and is transmitted by the prophet who is summoned to hear. A new exodus is to take place, even more wonderful than that from Egypt. It is certain because it is the fulfilment of the enduring word of God. The land of Judah will see the unmistakable evidence of God's presence once more, as he brings back his exiled people.

1–2. 'comfort'...'speak'...'tell': the verbs are plural imperatives. Who are being commanded? Early interpreters in the Targum understood this to be addressed to the prophets. The Septuagint adds the word 'priests' at the beginning of verse 2 and understands the commands as addressed to them. The use of the plural in Gen. 1: 26; 3: 22, and Isa. 6: 8 (Hebrew text) suggests that the words were addressed to the heavenly council waiting to receive the commands of God the King. This council is referred to in 1 Kings 22: 19–22; Jer. 23: 18, 22; Job 1: 6; 2: 1. It would be a natural image since an earthly king would have his council to inform and advise him and to receive his commands. While Israel's King does not need to be informed or advised, it would be appropriate for him to issue his commands to his council into which the prophet has been called. Verses 1–8 then may be read as the inaugural vision, or vocation of the prophet, similar to that of Isaiah in Isa. 6 or Ezekiel in Ezek. 1: 4 – 3: 11, although the divine word in this situation is not one of threat but of comfort. The Hebrew word for 'comfort' includes the sense of relief from distress, invigoration, restoration of courage. By implication it answers the anguished cry of those who mourned the devastated city in Lam. 1: 'no one to comfort' (five times).

'my people'...'your God': these words at once recall the covenant formula 'you shall be my people and I will be your God', especially as that formula was used by Jeremiah (Jer. 7: 23; 31: 33).

2. *speak tenderly:* literally, 'speak upon the heart'. The expression occurs eight times in the Old Testament; cp.

Gen. 50:21; Ruth 2:13 where also it is preceded by the word for
'comfort' (N.E.B. 'eased my mind'). It conveys the sense of
God's deep concern to reassure his people. *Jerusalem* is not so
much the geographical city as the people of God whom it
symbolizes (cp. 51:16), in whose midst God dwells. *term of
bondage*: originally 'military service' and so 'compulsory
service' as in Job 7:1. The reference is to the enforced exile
at the hands of the Babylonian Empire – but this is seen by the
prophet in a deeper sense. It was an act of God on account of
his people's iniquity (*penalty*). ('Iniquity' and 'penalty' are
the same word in Hebrew; each is involved in the other. Any
departure from, or infringement of, the covenant relationship
was to involve oneself in death.) In this situation the prophet
can declare what must have seemed impossible. God has
forgiven or discharged the penalty. This forgiveness includes
release from the enforced exile. *double measure* is not to be
taken in a prosaically literal sense; the prophet would not
imply that God is unjust. The exile was the inevitable consequence of sin as earlier prophets had warned.

3–5. *a voice that cries* apparently refers to a member of the
heavenly council who will act as herald of the King. The
message is doubly allusive. On the one hand it called to mind
the exodus from Egypt and the passage through the desert.
On the other it recalled what these exiles had so often seen,
namely the festal procession of the gods along the great
highway of Babylon. The language of verse 3 echoes the
words of the Babylonian hymn which contains the lines:

'Make his [Nabu's] way good, renew his road.
Make straight the path, hew out for him a track.'

It is possible that such processional hymns were familiar
to the prophet and his own words could be a challenge to
Babylonian religion. It is also possible that he is adapting to
this new exodus a hymn from before the exile to Israel's God
(cp. Ps. 68:7). But the herald has a message which far surpasses either event. There will be no tribulation as in the
exodus from Egypt, but a passage made smooth and level.

The processional way *for our God* will stretch right across the desert to Judaea, a *highway* that dwarfed the might of Babylon itself, as the *glory of the LORD* will surpass the magnificent images of Babylon's gods. Verse 5 hints at what will be developed later. The whole world of mankind will suddenly realize that the apparently defeated God of Israel is leading home his people in triumph. The closing sentence of verse 5 is like a solemn Amen, the significance of which can be understood in the light of 55: 11.

6–8. If we follow the N.E.B. it would appear that two members of the heavenly council are speaking, the one commanding the other to proclaim, 'Cry'; the other asking what he is to proclaim. This dialogue somewhat resembles the account in 1 Kings 22: 21, and is a reasonable translation of the Masoretic Text (the Hebrew text from which the Old Testament has been translated) with the addition of the word 'another'. Neither the ancient translations nor the Dead Sea Scrolls understood the verse in this way. With no alteration of the consonants, but a change of the vowel points, they read 'And I said' (cp. N.E.B. footnote *d*). If this is correct we now have the prophet's response to the mysterious command, apparently offering himself freely to the divine claim (cp. Isa. 6: 8). It may be argued that this solution is a temptingly easy way to deal with a difficult text; on the other hand the evidence is very early in the Jewish tradition. The footnote rendering has commended itself to most commentators, and they understand this passage as the prophet's call to prophesy.

The incredible good news of God's forgiveness of his guilty people to be actualized in a mighty act of salvation needs one thing more: a word of assurance. This is given in the words that follow, reaching the climax in the closing words of verse 8. We might sum it up in prose form: man's loyalty to God wavers and fades, but our God's word stands firm for ever. What the prophet will have to say may well sound incredible to the disillusioned and despairing exiles, but it is the sure and certain word, effective to accomplish the divine will in history. 'they last no longer': this replaces 'goodliness' or 'beauty', in the Authorized Version, the Revised Version, the Revised Standard Version and the Jerusalem Bible, neither of which translations does justice to the Hebrew word which elsewhere is translated as 'constant love' or the like. The point is not the transitoriness of man's life, but the feebleness of his devotion to God. If the charge against the Jews, however just, sounds unfeeling, we should recall that the prophet includes himself in the 'all mankind'. The fresh vegetation quickly dies when the hot, dry wind of early summer blows. So does man's devotion before the winds of adversity. But this wind is the breath of the LORD. When man acknowledges this, he can begin to receive the enduring promise of *our God*.

7. The words in the N.E.B. footnote are almost certainly a comment by an early scribe who recollects Ps. 90: 6.

8. *the word of our God* is the word, not only of the earlier prophets, but the covenant word, so often repeated in Israel's liturgies, which is the very foundation of Israel's life.

9–11. The imperatives here are feminine singular, as distinct from the plural of verse 1, and the masculine singular of verse 6. This may be understood as a collective verb, describing a band of prophets (*You who bring...good news*), also feminine (cp. 52: 7 though the messenger here is masculine singular), as apparently in the N.E.B. But since the pronouns and relative clause are all feminine singular the alternative translation in the N.E.B. footnotes *c* and *d* may be preferred. It may be that Jerusalem cannot be exhorted to go up *to the mountain-top* but, as in verse 2, Jerusalem may be understood not in a geographical sense, but as a symbolic term for Israel where God dwells. So the primary function of restored Israel is to proclaim to those who are in Judaea the triumphant coming of the LORD at the head of his restored people.

10 corresponds closely to the Gospel saying 'the kingdom of God is upon you' (Mark 1: 15). *recompense...reward:*

these are the exiled Jews whom the LORD brings with him, the fruits of his victory and evidence of his triumph.

11. *shepherd* is a royal title (cp. especially Ezek. 34: 11) but the LORD is a king who cares especially for the weak and defenceless. ✶

Israel delivered and redeemed

THE LORD THE CREATOR

Who has gauged the waters in the palm of his hand,   12
or with its span set limits to the heavens?
Who has held all the soil of earth in a bushel,
or weighed the mountains on a balance
   and the hills on a pair of scales?
Who has set limits to the spirit of the LORD?   13
What counsellor stood at his side to instruct him?
With whom did he confer to gain discernment?   14
Who taught him how to do justice[a]
   or gave him lessons in wisdom?
Why, to him nations are but drops from a bucket,   15
  no more than moisture on the scales;
coasts and islands weigh as light as specks of dust.
All Lebanon does not yield wood enough for fuel   16
or beasts enough for a sacrifice.
All nations dwindle to nothing before him,   17
he reckons them mere nothings, less than nought.

✶ It should be noted that it is only for the sake of convenience that we make a break at verse 17, since the whole chapter is

[a] *So Sept.; Heb. adds* and gave him lessons in knowledge.

a unity leading from a contemplation of Israel's God as Creator to him as Saviour. We shall do justice to the thought of the prophet only if we recognize this movement of thought. He is not arguing for the creative power of God. He is asserting that it is Israel's God, the LORD, who alone is Creator, and that is why the despairing group of exiles not only may but must await confidently his work of deliverance. The thought in this chapter is much more pointed than the simple affirmation that God is the Creator. First, it is addressed mainly to second-generation exiled Jews. That is to say, it is to people who have suffered the bitterness of defeat, which for the ancient world meant the defeat of their God. Doubtless they clung nostalgically to many of their ancient practices and traditions, but the most distinctive expressions of their religion could not be practised in 'a foreign land' (Ps. 137: 4), a land in which their God had no place, or at best a place subordinate to the victorious gods of Babylon. Secondly, these exiles were confronted by a religion whose temples and ritual practices far surpassed in magnificence anything that Jerusalem had known. Everything conspired to seduce these exiles from their ancient faith. It is against this human background that we can recognize the astonishing faith of the prophet, and understand the despair of the listeners (verse 27).

In the opening section we have a series of rhetorical questions (12-14) expecting the answer: 'No one!' Those who heard the prophet would inevitably think of the council of the gods who advised and supported the great god of Babylon, Marduk, as they are depicted in the Epic of Creation, but while the echoes can be heard, they serve but to emphasize the sole authority and sovereignty of Israel's God. It is a powerful argument presented, as is usual in the Old Testament, in the form of a poem (cp. Job 38-9), but an argument addressed to a concrete situation rather than an abstract discussion. Ultimately this and other passages in these chapters may be described as monotheistic; but that is inadequate. The point is that the LORD, Yahweh, God of Israel is uniquely the Creator.

22

12. *waters:* these are the waters of chaos which were literally put in their place by God (cp. Gen. 1: 6–10; Ps. 104: 6–9). *span* is the measurement from thumb-tip to little finger-tip of the spread hand, i.e. 8 inches or 20 cm. *bushel:* literally a third part of an ephah, about 12 litres. The measures referred to vividly indicate the total inadequacy of any human standards for describing the power of the Creator.

13. Unlike the supreme god of Babylon Israel's God needs no advisers. He is the all-wise as he is the all-powerful. *spirit of the LORD:* i.e. his mind and purpose, cp. the Septuagint, quoted by Paul in Rom. 11: 34.

14. *to do justice:* literally 'the way of justice' which might be understood as 'the right way', the best and most appropriate way in which the government of the world should be conducted. The Hebrew word for justice has a wider meaning than the corresponding English word.

15–17 describe God as the sole ruler of history. Verse 16 may be regarded as a parenthesis which describes even the most extravagant sacrifices as inadequate means of expressing man's worship. The might of empires and the pomp of kings are insignificant before the real majesty of God. ✳

THE INCOMPARABLE CREATOR AND SAVIOUR

What likeness will you find for God 18
or what form to resemble his?
Is it an image which a craftsman sets up, 19
and a goldsmith covers with plate
and fits[a] with studs of silver as a costly gift?
Or is it mulberry-wood that will not rot which a 20
man chooses,
seeking out a skilful craftsman for it,
to mount an image that will not fall?

[a] fits: so *Pesh.*; *Heb.* a goldsmith.

[6^a]   Each workman helps the others,
        each man encourages his fellow.

[7^a]   The craftsman urges on the goldsmith,
        the gilder urges the man who beats the anvil,
        he declares the soldering to be sound;
        he fastens the image with nails
        so that it will not fall down.

21   Do you not know, have you not heard,
        were you not told long ago,
        have you not perceived ever since the world began,

22   that God sits throned on the vaulted roof of earth,
            whose inhabitants are like grasshoppers^b?
        He stretches out the skies like a curtain,
        he spreads them out like a tent to live in;

23   he reduces the great to nothing
        and makes all earth's princes less than nothing.

24   Scarcely are they planted, scarcely sown,
        scarcely have they taken root in the earth,
            before he blows upon them and they wither away,
            and a whirlwind carries them off like chaff.

25   To whom then will you liken me,
            whom set up as my equal?
            asks the Holy One.

26   Lift up your eyes to the heavens;
        consider who created it all,
        led out their host one by one
        and called them all by their names;
            through his great might, his might and power,
            not one is missing.

[a] *These are verses 6 and 7 of ch. 41, transposed to this point.*
[b] *Or* locusts.

Why do you complain, O Jacob,   27
   and you, Israel, why do you say,
'My plight is hidden from the LORD
  and my cause has passed out of God's notice'?
Do you not know, have you not heard?   28
The LORD, the everlasting God, creator of the wide
      world,
    grows neither weary not faint;
    no man can fathom his understanding.
He gives vigour to the weary,   29
new strength to the exhausted.
Young men may grow weary and faint,   30
even in their prime they may stumble and fall;
but those who look to the LORD will win new strength, 31
they will grow wings like eagles;
they will run and not be weary,
they will march on and never grow faint.

✻ N.E.B. decision to include 41: 6–7 into this section is
reasonable, since these verses seem to have little connection
with 41: 5 or with anything in ch. 41. On the other hand, 40:
19f. fits uneasily into ch. 40 and only appears as an 'answer'
to 40: 18 by a translation which the present Hebrew text
hardly justifies. It is possible that the passage 40: 19–20 + 41:
6–7 is connected with 44: 9–11, where in verses 9f. the same
word for image occurs. (Others would transfer 40: 19–20 to
40: 5.) Then 40: 18 would serve well as an introduction to
40: 21. The intervening verses 41: 6–7 might be taken as a
somewhat awkward parenthesis, or misplaced from 44:
9–11.

  The point of the parenthesis is clear and we may take it
first. On the one hand it recalls and reinforces the commandment of Exod. 20: 4 which was regularly recited in Israel's

great acts of worship. On the other it points to the spectacle of Babylonian religion. There is a touch of irony in the words 'fall' and 'fall down'. What kind of a god is this who needs support?

19–20. Literally, 'an image – a craftsman casts it and a goldsmith covers it with gold and casts silver chains'. The word for *goldsmith* and the second 'casts' are the same in Hebrew, hence N.E.B. footnotes; 'silver chains' (N.E.B. *studs of silver*) occurs only here although a similar word appears in 1 Kings 6: 21 as 'chains'. Presumably the chains were attached to something to hold the image firmly in place. *costly gift* has been taken from a word in verse 20 (Revised Standard Version 'an offering').

The Hebrew text of these verses is difficult to translate as a comparison between the N.E.B. and earlier versions will indicate. It seems clear that the text has suffered in the course of transmission, partly because of the occurrence of words whose precise meaning had been forgotten, e.g. *mulberry-wood* (the N.E.B. may be accepted). The general sense is clear. The image was first carved from a hard wood, then covered with gold plating and either ornamented with silver studs or fastened with silver chains to a post or a wall so that it was held firmly in place. The subtle irony of the description is obvious, all the more in that it is an accurate description of idol-making as told by the Babylonians themselves. How could any Jew respect, let alone worship, a god of whom such an image was a symbolic representation!

The argument of verses 18 and 21–31 is clear and particularly skilful. There is nothing in heaven or earth that can compare with Him who is the 'Holy One' whom Israel from ancient time has known as Yahweh. Can these exiled Jews really suppose that he has overlooked their plight? Let them recall his inexhaustible power and wisdom, and with renewed faith find again for themselves those infinite resources. The poet begins first with the situation which confronts the exiles (verses 18, 21–4), then he moves directly into Israel's faith (verses 25, 26) and from this foundation addresses himself to the exiles' little faith (verses 27–31).

18. *God* represents the Hebrew *'El*, a word used in the days before the exile for the High God of the Canaanites and identified with Yahweh. But it is also the equivalent for the Babylonian word for 'god' (the word *God* in verse 22 has been added by the translators). Thus the opening section would be equivalent to the question 'What do you mean, Jews, living in a pagan environment, when you say "God"? That he is the sole creator and ruler is, or should be, common ground if the word God means anything at all.' The argument is similar to Rom. 1: 19f.; Acts 17: 26. It is not the appeal to revelation but to natural theology.

22–4 sound like a quotation from a hymn using participles, and the clauses really begin with 'he who sits enthroned ...spreading out...reducing...'. *less than nothing* as in verse 17 is the word used in Gen. 1: 2: 'without form'.

25–6. Now the poet turns specifically to the Jewish exiles with the word *Holy One*. The Creator is not merely God, he is the God of Israel, he whom his people have known in their history and experience (cp. Ps. 22: 3f.). The opening question is the same as verse 18 but with the specific title *the Holy One*. *who created it all* should be read as a question, 'Who created these?', i.e. the stars. Here the reference is to the stars understood by the Babylonians as the rulers of human destiny. For the Jew they are God's creatures and entirely under his control.

27–31 is the climax of the argument, as the poet speaks directly to the condition of the exiles. Now the great name of Israel's God is used, the LORD, i.e. Yahweh, he who has revealed himself as the deliverer from Egypt. Thus in Hebrew verse 27 reads 'my God's notice' rather than *God's notice*. *everlasting:* i.e. throughout the history of mankind.

29. *He gives* is again a participle as though quoting a hymn.

30. *Young men...their prime:* there is gentle irony here. The words are appropriate to those who would normally be called to fight. That is precisely what they cannot do. There

is to be no battle for freedom. The one certain hope for the future lies in the LORD who will transform a defeated and hopeless nation into a strong and tireless people of God. ✶

THE SOVEREIGN LORD OF HISTORY

✶ With ch. 41 after the poetic introduction, prophecy begins. God speaks through the prophet to declare the real meaning of the world-shaking events that are taking place. The reference is to the amazing successes of Cyrus who with such remarkable rapidity had conquered the kingdoms to the north and west of Mesopotamia, and now is poised for the conquest of Babylonia itself. The form of the prophecy is that of the law courts. All the nations of the world, including Babylon, are summoned to hear the evidence and to give their judgement. Who is doing this? It is none other than the LORD. It is certainly not the great gods of Babylon. It may be noted that the chapter falls into five sections: verses 1–5, 8–10, 11–16, 17–20, 21–9. Except for verses 17–20, which have no obvious connection with the rest of the chapter, the sections are closely related, the opening and closing law-court scenes providing the background for the two encouraging words to Israel. The gods, and therefore their peoples, are proved to be impotent; Israel, the people of him who is at this very moment of history demonstrating his sovereign power, has every reason for confidence. ✶

THE VICTOR'S PROGRESS

41   Keep silence before me, all you coasts and islands;
  let the peoples come to meet me.[a]
  Let them come near, then let them speak;
  we will meet at the place of judgement, I and they.

[a] come to meet me: *prob. rdg., transposing, with slight change, from end of verse 5; Heb.* win new strength (*repeated from 40: 31*).

Tell me, who raised up that one from the east,   2
one greeted by victory wherever he goes?
Who is it that puts nations into his power
and makes kings go down before him,*a*
he scatters them with his sword like dust
and with his bow like chaff before the wind;
he puts them to flight and passes on unscathed,   3
swifter than any traveller on foot?
Whose work is this, I ask, who has brought it to   4
       pass?
Who has summoned the generations from the
       beginning?
It is I, the Lord, I am the first,
and to the last of them I am He.
Coasts and islands saw it and were afraid,   5
     the world trembled from end to end.*b*

✭ The nations of the world are summoned to a solemn
assembly to judge for themselves who is responsible for the
victories of Cyrus. It is probable that these words were spoken
when news reached Babylon of the defeat of Croesus, king
of Lydia, Babylon's most powerful ally. It is to be noted that
it is not the gods who are summoned, but the nations. The
gods are incapable of speech because they are lifeless, but the
nations are able to judge for themselves. There seem to be
echoes in this passage of Ps. 96.

1. *Keep silence:* the excited clamour of the crowd, as
rumours and reports of Cyrus' progress are received, is
silenced and men are summoned to hear the Lord and form a
true judgement on the world situation. *coasts and islands:*
literally the nations of the Mediterranean, the people of Syria

[a] before him: *prob. rdg.; Heb. om.*
[b] *See note on verse 1.*

and Phoenicia, here meaning all peoples even to the world's utmost limit (cp. verse 5).

2. *one from the east:* i.e. Cyrus, who began as king of Persia to the south-east of Mesopotamia, overthrew the Median king to the north (verse 25) and then invaded Asia Minor, where Lydia was the most important kingdom at this time. *greeted by victory wherever he goes:* cp. the Revised Standard Version. This is a difficult sentence in Hebrew and many alternative translations have been offered. *victory* is literally 'righteousness', but this means the fulfilment of God's righteous purpose, and must be represented here by *victory* as in verse 10 and 46: 13. The rhetorical questions, with the answer in verse 4, affirm the sovereignty of Israel's God.

3. *unscathed:* literally 'in peace' but the Hebrew *shalom* has a much wider meaning than the English 'peace' and includes the meaning of complete security. These two verses draw attention to what all would feel to be the miraculous successes of Cyrus.

4. For the prophet they were miraculous since they pointed men to the LORD. Doubtless Cyrus would have attributed his victories to Ahura Mazda who was the supreme deity of Persian religion and remained as the sole deity in the religion of Zoroaster, but the prophet will go on to say that these victories will lead to the deliverance of Israel, and must therefore be the work of Israel's God. He is the lord of history, there at the beginning and also at the end.

5. This is the conclusion of the case. The nations at last see who it is who rules all human destiny. ✴

FEAR NOT

8[a]
> But you, Israel my servant,
> you, Jacob whom I have chosen,
>   race of Abraham my friend,

[a] *Verses 6 and 7 transposed to follow 40: 20.*

I have taken you up,   9
have fetched you from the ends of the earth,
    and summoned you from its farthest corners,
I have called you my servant,
have chosen you and not cast you off:
fear nothing, for I am with you;   10
be not afraid, for I am your God.
I strengthen you, I help you,
I support you with my victorious right hand.

✳ The divine word is now addressed to Israel. The news of the victories of Cyrus would in themselves give little comfort to the exiles. The threatened collapse of the Babylonian Empire could only mean a change of masters. But Israel ought to understand these events at a deeper level as soon as it is recognized that this is the LORD's work. So this word is first a reminder of the ancient promises. The language recalls the concluding words of assurance in many of the Psalms which speak of distress and suffering, e.g. Ps. 44. So these world-shaking events are the prelude to God's work of deliverance for his people.

8. *Israel my servant*: although the word is addressed immediately to the exiles, it is inclusive of all Israel. Israel is God's *servant*, that is, the one who owes total loyalty and obedience to him who can be confidently expected to protect. It also includes the idea of worshipper. The concept of all Israel as the servant of the LORD is one of the characteristic terms of this prophet, as is *I have chosen*.

race of Abraham my friend: race is not used in the modern sense, and could be rendered 'descendants'. It is surprising how infrequent are the references in the prophets to Abraham, none in the prophets before the exile except Isa. 29: 22. But in the exile these ancient traditions acquired a deeper significance as they recalled God's age-long devotion to his people.

31

my friend is literally 'who loved me'; cp. 2 Chron. 20: 7; Jas. 2: 23. *have fetched you:* since this follows on the reference to Abraham it may be an allusion to his call to leave his country and kindred (Gen. 12: 1), but this hardly suits the present context. The allusion may be to the exodus from Egypt or the exile from Judah. If it is the latter it would be a complete reversal of what the exiles supposed. Nebuchadnezzar had been the Lord's servant (Jer. 25: 9) to bring Israel among the heathen where the divine purpose would be fulfilled. Therefore *fear nothing* indeed! *

IN GOD IS YOUR HOPE

11   Now shall all who defy you
      be disappointed and put to shame;
      all^a who set themselves against you
      shall be as nothing; they shall vanish.

12   You will look for your assailants but not find
            them;
      all who take up arms against you
      shall be as nothing, nothing at all.

13   For I, the LORD your God,
      take you by the right hand;
      I say to you, Do not fear;
      it is I who help you,

14   fear not, Jacob you worm and Israel poor louse.
      It is I who help you, says the LORD,
            your ransomer, the Holy One of Israel.

15   See, I will make of you a sharp threshing-sledge,
            new and studded with teeth;
      you shall thresh the mountains and crush them
      and reduce the hills to chaff;

[a] all: *so Scroll; Heb. om.*

32

you shall winnow them, the wind shall carry them   16
  away
and a great gale shall scatter them.
Then shall you rejoice in the LORD
  and glory in the Holy One of Israel.

---

* This oracle relates to the future, and tells of Israel's triumph over all who would resist. Again there are echoes from the concluding assurances in the psalms of lament; cp. Ps. 35: 26.

11. *all who defy you* is probably a quite general reference, although it might refer specifically to Babylon. *defy:* literally 'be hot with anger against', as also at 45: 24. *set themselves against you:* the Hebrew word means 'those who bring a charge against you in court'.

13. *take you by the right hand:* there is a two-fold reference here. The first is to a part of the ritual in the Babylonian New Year ceremony, in which the king took the right hand of Marduk. The second is to the faith of Israel, finely expressed in Ps. 73: 23 and frequently in the Psalter. It is the sure grasp of God that makes it possible to say *Do not fear.*

14–16. There are features in these verses which suggest that they were originally an independent oracle. The Hebrew phrase for 'says the LORD' suggests a salvation oracle. The pronoun 'you', 'your' in verses 14 and 15*a* are feminine singular, while from 15*b* to 16 ('you shall thresh') they are masculine singular. The reason for the change is not obvious, but may be explained by the fact that the Hebrew for 'worm' is feminine while that for 'threshing-sledge' is masculine. The closing phrases in verse 16 are reminiscent of the Psalms that celebrate the rule of God.

14. *ransomer:* this is one of the most distinctive words in these chapters. It occurs twelve times and the corresponding verb six times. It is a technical term for one who has the sacred duty to rescue his kinsman from slavery (Lev. 25: 25), to buy back the property that has been alienated (Lev. 25: 23–5),

to avenge the death of the kinsman (Num. 35: 12). The word is used of Boaz in Ruth 2: 20; 3: 9 ('next-of-kin'). So in Second Isaiah God describes himself as the powerful member of the family who accepts the sacred obligation to come to the help of, and protect, his people in their extremity. The word is then associated with the phrase *the Holy One of Israel* which, paradoxically, emphasizes God's transcendence and aweful majesty (thirteen times in Second Isaiah). The God of incalculable power who is immeasurably beyond our grasp comes near to save; cp. Exod. 6: 6 'redeem'.

15. *sharp threshing-sledge:* the threshing-sledge was a heavy wooden board studded with sharp stones or iron. It is probable that the word for 'sharp', which also means 'threshing-sledge', has been added later to explain the uncommon word used by the prophet (occurring elsewhere only in 2 Sam. 24: 22; 1 Chron. 21: 23).

The function of the threshing-sledge was to beat out the grain from the stalks. The whole was then tossed into the air with shovels so that the wind could carry away the chaff and the heavier grain would fall to the ground. So the contemptible worm (verse 14) is transformed into a powerful threshing-sledge, capable of crushing mountains! These *mountains* and *hills* may represent the proud and arrogant nations (as Mic. 4: 13) or, more generally, any obstruction to the work of liberation as in 40: 4.

16. *a great gale:* the Hebrew word also means 'spirit' (cp. Gen. 1: 2 and footnote). In both, the incalculable divine energy is to be seen (cp. John 3: 8). ✷

THE DESERT TRANSFORMED

17   The wretched and the poor look for water and find
      none,
      their tongues are parched with thirst;
      but I the LORD will give them an answer,
      I, the God of Israel, will not forsake them.

I will open rivers among the sand-dunes 18
   and wells in the valleys;
I will turn the wilderness into pools
and dry land into springs of water;
I will plant cedars in the wastes, 19
and acacia and myrtle and wild olive;
the pine shall grow on the barren heath
side by side with fir and box,
that men may see and know, 20
may once for all give heed and understand
that the LORD himself has done this,
   that the Holy One of Israel has performed it.

✻ This salvation oracle is almost in parenthesis between verses 16 and 21. It opens abruptly with a description of a march of the liberated people through the desert which is miraculously transformed into a fertile land. It is not addressed directly to the exiles, but looks to the future when the liberated exiles will march through the wilderness to the holy land; cp. 43: 19–21. The oracle may be seen as a divine answer to those who were understandably fearful of the dangers of the journey. It is expressed in the familiar form of an answer to prayer for deliverence; cp. Ps. 107: 33–5. The language calls to mind the ancient recital of the wilderness wandering; but this occasion will be more wonderful than the journey from Egypt to Canaan, for the desert will be transformed into a paradise. The desert, the place of death and demons, will be transformed by the life-giving God.

17. Perhaps only those who have lived under conditions of drought can appreciate the intensity of feeling in this verse. The divine answer comes to those who are at the point of death.

20. The four verbs emphasize the function of miracle; it is that men may *know* God. *performed*: the Hebrew word is

35

that which appears in Gen. 1: 'created'. This work of salvation is a new creation. ✿

LORD OF THE PAST AND THE FUTURE

21 Come, open your plea, says the LORD,
    present your case, says Jacob's King;
       let them come forward, these idols,
22   let them foretell the future.
      Let them declare the meaning of past events
         that we may give our minds to it;
      let them predict things that are to be
         that we may know their outcome.
23   Declare what will happen hereafter;
      then we shall know you are gods.
      Do what you can, good or ill,
         anything that may grip us with fear and awe.
24   You cannot! You are sprung from nothing,
      your works are rotten;
      whoever chooses you is vile as you are.
25   I roused one from the north, and he obeyed;
      I called one from the east, summoned him in[a] my
           name,
      he marches over viceroys as if they were mud,
      like a potter treading his clay.
26 Tell us, who declared this from the beginning, that
         we might know it,
      or told us beforehand so that we could say, 'He was
         right'?
  Not one declared, not one foretold,
      not one heard a sound from you.

      [a] summoned him in: *or* who will call on.

Here is one who will speak[a] first as advocate for Zion, 27
    here I appoint defending counsel for Jerusalem;
but from the other side no advocate steps forward　　28
    and, when I look, there is no one there.
I ask a question and no one answers;
    see what empty things they are!　　29
        Nothing that they do has any worth,
        their effigies are wind, mere nothings.

✣ In these verses the scene is again that with which the
chapter began, a trial. But this time it is the so-called gods
whom the LORD challenges. Further, the challenge is greater.
Who is it who has controlled all past events and so given them
meaning? Who is it who is at work already to bring about the
future, so that men can meet what will happen with confidence? And if this goes beyond what any reasonable Babylonian could expect of the gods, so much the worse for them.
For this is precisely what Israel could and should expect,
from the very first proclamation of the divine name Yahweh.
Yet this is not an abstract argument; the test is quite practical.
Has any of the gods, even Nabu the god of prophecy, given
any warning of the victorious career of Cyrus and the imminent collapse of the Babylonian Empire which should be
very much the concern of the gods of Babylon? This is
precisely what the God of Israel has done. The case rests! This
is not a philosophical argument for monotheism, but a
religious and practical argument for the sole sovereignty of
Yahweh, who is the Lord of history.

21. *case:* literally strong things, convincing proofs.

22. *the future:* literally 'what will meet us'. *past events:*
probably refers particularly to the career of Cyrus although
in 43: 9 the same word is translated 'all that has gone before'
and means past history in a more general sense. *we…our…*

[a] one who will speak: *so Scroll; Heb. unintelligible.*

37

throughout the passage refers to the LORD and his people or possibly the heavenly council (cp. Ps. 82: 1).

23. The verse is an ironical cry of desperation. It is the proper business of the gods to reveal the future by the prophets and to bring about good fortune or ill.

24. But in fact nothing comes from them. They are quite impotent. Therefore those who worship such gods are as 'loathsome as the thing (they) loved' (Hos. 9: 11).

25. *one from the north*...*one from the east:* the allusion is to Cyrus, whose conquest of the Medes gave him a kingdom north (Media) and east (Persia) of Mesopotamia. *summoned*... *in my name:* the translation, as the footnote shows, is not certain. The footnote translates the Hebrew text which suggests that Cyrus will recognize that it is Israel's God who has given him the victory. There is no evidence that Cyrus acknowledged the LORD, except in the Hebrew version of Cyrus' decree in 2 Chron. 36: 23; Ezra 1: 2–4, and this is clearly an interpretation of the Aramaic version in Ezra 6: 3–5. It may seem improbable that Cyrus would invoke the god of the Jewish exiles. The nearest parallel is the statement in the Cyrus Cylinder where the king acknowledges the gods of Babylon. (The Cyrus Cylinder is a broken cylinder discovered in the nineteenth century, now in the British Museum, in which Cyrus describes himself as the divinely appointed deliverer of Babylon from the corrupt and oppressive rule of Nabonidus. It also describes Cyrus' intention to restore to their native lands war-captives and the temple statues of gods.) The Dead Sea Scroll reads 'and he called him by his name' and this may indicate that the Hebrew text is not clear. The N.E.B. text, based on a slight emendation, may be regarded as probable, and is supported by 45: 3. Otherwise we must regard the prophetic assertion in the footnote as hyperbole like the transformation of the desert into a paradise in verses 18–19. *viceroys* is a Babylonian word used in Jer. 51: 23, 57.

26. The gods are challenged again: who has predicted the victories of Cyrus so that the witness can say *He was right*?

There was neither prediction nor fulfilment. There was, as we know, plenty of prediction among the Babylonian seers but about this all-important event there was silence.

27–8. The N.E.B. provides not only a translation of the obscure Hebrew text, based on the Dead Sea Scroll of Isaiah, but an interpretation. The Hebrew text, even in the Scroll, appears to be so obscure that a sure translation is not possible. The N.E.B. interpretation may be regarded as probable but not certain; it makes good sense and suits the context. *defending counsel* renders a word which means 'bring news' (40: 9) and the N.E.B. has supplied *advocate* and *defending*. It is possible that the prophet's word meant:

> (27) In the beginning I have brought news to Zion
>   and appointed a messenger for Jerusalem.
> (28) I looked but there was no one
>   and from these there was none to counsel. ✲

GOD'S CHOSEN INSTRUMENT

Here is my servant, whom I uphold,   **42**
my chosen one in whom I delight,
I have bestowed my spirit upon him,
and he will make justice shine on the nations.
He will not call out or lift his voice high,   2
or*a* make himself heard in the open street.
He will not break a bruised reed,   3
or snuff out a smouldering wick;
he will make justice shine on every race,*b*
never faltering, never breaking down,*c*   4
he will plant justice on earth,
while coasts and islands wait for his teaching.

[a] He will not...or: *or* In very truth he will call out and lift his voice high, and...   [b] on every race: *or* in truth.
[c] never faltering...down: *or* he will neither rebuke nor wound.

✲ This is the first Servant Poem.

The interpretation of this and the three subsequent Servant Poems will be based on the understanding that the Servant is Israel in the purpose of God. For other interpretations see pp. 10–14. We have noted that the interest of these poems is not in who the Servant is, but in what he does and in how he does it. In this poem the key word is 'justice' (verses 1, 3 and 4). At once we are confronted with the problem of translation. 'Justice', in Hebrew and in English, is a law-court term. It is what the judge brings into effect when some wrong has been done. In Israel it is an integral part of the covenant relationship. So the aim of justice is to set right whatever has harmed the relationship between God and his people, and therefore whatever destroys or threatens to destroy the welfare of the covenant community. Justice is what God requires, and brings into effect. It is therefore more than a legal term; so in English 'to do a man justice' is 'to be fair to a man' and this goes beyond what is legally just.

In the Old Testament the word may be used of the whole way of life appropriate to those who are loyal to God, including worship and conduct (cp. Jer. 5: 4–5; N.E.B. 'ordinances'). Thus the function of the Servant is to make evident to all mankind the will of God, in order that men may know him and fulfil his royal purposes in loyal trust and obedience. Perhaps no one word is adequate, unless we think of justice in the religion of the Bible which includes the conduct and worship that God requires.

1. *uphold* is also used of God's servant in 41: 10 (N.E.B. 'support'). *my chosen one* is used of the Davidic king in Ps. 89: 4 and of Israel in Isa. 45: 4. The meaning is 'one who has been chosen for a special task'. The emphasis is on the divine choice, not on any aptitude or qualities of the one chosen. *bestowed my spirit:* it is recognized that the task is beyond the normal strength or ability of man. It can be accomplished only by the endowment of divine power. In days before the exile the gift of the spirit is normally associated with the Davidic

king, the LORD's anointed (cp. Isa. 11: 2). *make justice shine:* the coming of justice is likened to the dawn of a new day (cp. Ps. 19: 4*b*–5), similarly in verse 3.

2. The sevenfold negative in verses 2–4 suggests a contrast. This contrast may be with the usual royal proclamation of kings on their accession, or with Cyrus in particular.

3. *on every race:* the footnote translates the Masoretic Text. The text supposes different vowels but the same consonants.

4. *teaching:* the Hebrew word is *torah*, the giving of which was normally the function of the priest (Deut. 33: 10), although occasionally of the prophet (Isa. 1: 10). The reference may be to Israel as the 'kingdom of priests' (Exod. 19: 6). Some have understood this passage as referring to Cyrus, but this seems improbable. ✵

THE SALVATION OF THE WORLD

Thus speaks the LORD who is God,   5
   he who created the skies and stretched them out,
   who fashioned the earth and all that grows in it,
who gave breath to its people,
   the breath of life to all who walk upon it:
I, the LORD, have called you with righteous purpose   6
   and taken you by the hand;
   I have formed you, and appointed you
   to be a light*a* to all peoples,
   a beacon for the nations,
   to open eyes that are blind,   7
to bring captives out of prison,
   out of the dungeons where they lie in darkness.
I am the LORD; the LORD*b* is my name;   8
   I will not give my glory to another god,
   nor my praise to any idol.

[*a*] *Or* a covenant.   [*b*] the LORD: *or* He.

41

9   See how the first prophecies have come to pass,
       and now I declare new things;
   before they break from the bud I announce them to
       you.

✵ While there are difficulties in detail about the interpretation of this passage (see below) the main theme is clear. 'You' (second person singular) are to be the agent of the divine purpose for all peoples. To this end 'you' have been appointed by the LORD who is the Creator of the world of nature and mankind, the only true God. Some would see these verses as the continuation of the Servant Poem, but the introductory words and the change of person would suggest that this is a new oracle and the context would indicate that, in the mind of the prophet, it is a particular explanation of the role of the Servant. Others have regarded 'you' as Cyrus (cp. 45: 1f.), but the words of verse 6 hardly seem appropriate to a military conqueror however liberal his declared policy. While therefore certainty cannot be claimed, we may see these verses as a new oracle describing the universal mission of the Servant Israel, an amazing fulfilment of its royal and priestly function.

5. The verse opens with the conventional formula of a royal message, *the LORD who is God*; *God* translates the Hebrew *'El* rather than the more common *'Elohim*, and among the prophets is characteristic of these chapters, as it is of the Psalms (cp. Isa. 40: 18). In this prophet it may be deliberate since it resembles the Babylonian word for god and would convey the meaning 'the true God, Yahweh'. *he who created:* the relative pronoun corresponds to a participle, as also in the following verbs, and is characteristic of the hymn, as in the Hebrew of Ps. 136: 4-7. The creative activity of God is a frequent theme in these chapters.

6. *with righteous purpose:* literally 'with righteousness'. The same word is used in 41: 2, 10, and so here might be

rendered 'victoriously', i.e. to fulfil the divine purpose in the salvation of all mankind. *to be a light to all peoples:* the word translated *to be a light* usually means 'for (as) a covenant'. It is possible that the word may be derived from another root, hence the N.E.B. rendering. Certainly the expression 'appointed you to be a covenant' is unique. Nevertheless the older translation (see the N.E.B. footnote) is possible and the phrase could mean that God has appointed the Servant to be, like the divided animal (Gen. 15: 17; Jer. 34: 18), the instrument of the covenant he will make with all mankind. The metaphor is admittedly unusual, but in the light of Isa. 53 not impossible. The Servant is to be, not like Moses the mediator of the covenant, but the means whereby the new covenant will be made, and so a light (*beacon*) *for the nations.*

7. If the interpretation of verse 6 be accepted then this verse is not a reference to the exiles, who in any case were not imprisoned, but to the pagan nations who will be freed from their spiritual blindness and chains. This is the 'righteous' work of God, whereby (verse 8) he will be recognized as the only true God.

9. *first prophecies:* literally 'former things'. While this may refer to prophecies before the exile, it could refer to the saving work of God in the exodus. This is now to issue, miraculously, in a new work of salvation for all men. This is the future made known to *you* (plural), the exiles. ✳

A SONG OF VICTORY

Sing a new song to the LORD,
>   sing his praise throughout the earth,
>   you that sail the sea, and all sea-creatures,
>   and you that inhabit the coasts and islands.*[a]*

10

[a] you that sail…islands: or, *with slight change,* let the sea and all that is in it, the coasts and islands, echo his praise.

11   Let the wilderness and its towns rejoice,
           and the villages of the tribe of Kedar.
    Let those who live in Sela shout for joy
           and cry out from the hill-tops.

12   You coasts and islands, all uplift his praises;
           let all ascribe glory to the LORD.

13   The LORD will go forth as a warrior,
           he will rouse the frenzy of battle like a hero;
           he will shout, he will raise the battle-cry
           and triumph over his foes.

14   Long have I lain still,
           I kept silence and held myself in check;
           now I will cry like a woman in labour,
               whimpering, panting and gasping.

15   I will lay waste mountains and hills
           and shrivel all their green herbs;
           I will turn rivers into desert wastes*a*
           and dry up all the pools.

16   Then will I lead blind men on their way*b*
           and guide them by paths they do not know;
    I will turn darkness into light before them
           and straighten their twisting roads.
    All this I will do and leave nothing undone.

17   Those who trust in an image,
           those who take idols for their gods
           turn tail in bitter shame.

* With great artistry the prophet leaves the reader of 42: 1–9
with the incredible message he has received, and directs his

[a] desert wastes: *prob. rdg.; Heb.* coasts and islands.
[b] *Prob. rdg.; Heb. adds* which they do not know.

thoughts to him who alone can bring these things to pass. What follows is 'a new song' (cp. Pss. 33: 3; 96: 1; 98: 1), which is to be sung by the whole of mankind, to whom the light has come. This is to replace the hymns with which the New Year was celebrated, for it is in fact a new world order that is to be celebrated. The song will be sung by all mankind and all creation.

10. *you that sail the sea:* many, by a small emendation, would read the footnote. There is no textual justification for this but it would be supported by Ps. 98: 7. The sea would then be the all-encompassing waters from which God had separated the inhabited earth.

11. *Kedar...Sela:* the reference is to Arabian tribes settled at the oases. *Sela* may be identified with Petra though recent archaeological work suggests that this is not so; both words mean 'rock'. But Sela may be a descriptive word for any craggy district.

13. *as a warrior:* this alludes to the song in Exod. 15, especially verse 3. The themes of a new creation and a new act of deliverance are combined. The *foes* are both the cosmic powers (cp. 51: 9f.), and the human oppressors.

14. The complaint of the exiles was that God was apparently indifferent to their distress (cp. Ps. 35: 22). But the *silence* was not indifference. God had restrained himself until the time was at hand for the rebirth of his people. With a violent change of simile, the warrior is now seen as a woman in childbirth.

15. First the old world order, which is typified in the Babylonian Empire, must be destroyed. The old certainties (*mountains, hills, rivers*) will go.

16. Then the exiles (the *blind*) will be led as in the first exodus, to their true home. *All this I will do:* literally 'These are the words', a good illustration of the word as something done as well as spoken (cp. 55: 11). *leave nothing undone* or 'I will not forsake them', i.e. either the words or the exiles.

17. A final word of judgement on the Babylonian Empire

and perhaps a warning to the exiles who might be tempted
to forsake the living God. ✳

THE BLIND AND DEAF SERVANT

18   Hear now, you that are deaf;
        you blind men, look and see:
19   yet who is blind but my servant,
        who so deaf as the messenger whom I send?
        Who so blind as the one who holds my
                commission,
            so deaf[a] as the servant of the LORD?
20   You have seen much but remembered little,
        your ears are wide open but nothing is heard.
21   It pleased the LORD, for the furtherance of his
                justice,
        to make his law a law of surpassing majesty;
22   yet here is a people plundered and taken as prey,
        all of them ensnared, trapped in holes,
            lost to sight in dungeons,
        carried off as spoil without hope of rescue,
        as plunder with no one to say, 'Give it back.'
23   Hear this, all of you who will,
        listen henceforward and give me a hearing:
        who gave away Jacob for plunder,
24   who gave Israel away for spoil?
        Was it not the LORD? They[b] sinned against him,
        they would not follow his ways
            and refused obedience to his law;
25   so in his anger he poured out upon Jacob
        his wrath and the fury of battle.

[a] deaf: *so some MSS.; others* blind.   [b] *So Targ.; Heb.* We.

46

It wrapped him in flames, yet still he did not learn
the lesson,
scorched him, yet he did not lay it to heart.

✻ Israel is addressed in a series of penetrating questions which
expose a lack of understanding of God's purpose in spite of
the words of the prophets (cp. Ezek. 12: 2). The present
condition of the exiles is not merely political, the result of
imperial aggression. Nor is it enough to say that it is a
punishment for sin. It is an act of God; and it is in order that
Israel may understand, and become, in fact, the LORD's
servant and messenger.

The obvious difficulty is that of relating this passage to 42:
1-4. The contradiction is more apparent than real. It is
characteristic of Israel's faith to state first, and emphatically,
the divine purpose for Israel and then equally emphatically
Israel's failure or even refusal to accept this purpose. Thus
Israel is God's son and his people (Exod. 3: 7; 4: 22) even
though the rest of the Exodus narrative states that Israel
murmured and was ungrateful and rebellious. The Israelites
are still God's sons and 'my own people' although they have
rebelled and cannot discern (Isa. 1: 2-3). So in this passage
Israel is described as quite unworthy of the high calling to be
the LORD's servant and messenger, yet it was the divine
purpose to choose this people to be his servant; and the purpose of God cannot be nullified even by Israel's unfitness for
the task. We may go further and say there was already one,
the prophet himself, who was responding in loyal obedience
to the divine purpose, whose life was permeating the life
of his people, in order that Israel might enter upon its true
role. Hence this series of questions to arouse the exiles in order
that they may share in what the prophet so confidently sees.

19. The verse expresses the grief and astonishment that it is
my servant and *messenger* who is blind and deaf (cp. Isa. 1: 2-3).
who holds my commission represents one word in Hebrew, elsewhere appearing as a personal name Meshullam (2 Kings 22: 3).

47

The exact meaning is uncertain but it must be similar to *my servant* or *messenger*.

21. *for the furtherance of his justice:* literally 'for his righteousness' sake'. The meaning is 'in order to bring about his victory (over sin and evil)'. *law:* perhaps 'teaching' in the sense of divine revelation would be better. Many would regard this verse as a later addition in the spirit of Ps. 119. If the *law* is interpreted as 'the Torah' then it must be admitted that the verse is intrusive. But if the above interpretation is accepted, the verse may belong to this prophetic oracle.

22. The language of this verse may seem exaggerated, since the evidence shows that the exiled Jews at this period had considerable freedom and lived in their own houses. But the language may be understood as the conventional language of the lament; cp. Ps. 102: 20.

23. *me* has been added, probably correctly, as referring to the prophet.

24. *They*, as the N.E.B. footnote *b* shows, is an emendation to produce a smoother reading. But 'We' may be correct to indicate the prophet's sense of solidarity with his people, even in their sin. The confession is what the prophet seeks from his people. Then they will rightly interpret the exile. ✻

YOUR DELIVERER

43 But now this is the word of the LORD,
     the word of your creator, O Jacob,
        of him who fashioned you, Israel:
     Have no fear; for I have paid your ransom;
     I have called you by name and you are my own.
2 When you pass through deep waters, I am with you,
        when you pass through rivers,
           they will not sweep you away;
        walk through fire and you will not be scorched,
        through flames and they will not burn you.

For I am the LORD your God, 3
the Holy One of Israel, your deliverer;
for your ransom I give Egypt,
Nubia and Seba are your price.
You are more precious to me than the Assyrians, 4
you are honoured and I have loved you,
I would give the Edomites in exchange for you,
and the Leummim for your life.

✫ In contrast to the preceding verses we now have an oracle of salvation. The words are addressed to Israel as to an individual.

1. *creator...fashioned...paid your ransom...called you by name:* these are all verbs in Hebrew and highly allusive. The same creative act that brought into being the heavens and the earth, created you. He who fashioned man ('formed' in Gen. 2: 7) fashioned you. He has now acted as your next-of-kin (paid your ransom) and addressed you as his covenant people.

2 calls to mind the thanksgiving hymn in Ps. 66 (especially verse 12). The *deep waters* and *rivers* would recall the exodus and entry into Canaan. *When* and 'For' (verse 3) translate a Hebrew particle which could correspond to English quotation marks. In that case the sentences in verse 2 would be quotations from a known prayer, followed by the great affirmation in verse 3.

3. *Egypt, Nubia, Seba* would correspond to the modern Egypt and Ethiopia. From the point of view of Israel this meant all Africa. While it may have been Persian policy to conquer Africa (and Egypt was conquered by Cyrus' son Cambyses), it is probable that the prophet was simply saying 'the farthest parts of the world' (cp. verses 5–6).

4. *than the Assyrians:* the N.E.B. has emended the vowels in a word which as it stands means 'because'. This is attractive since the passage would lead one to expect the name of a

people. Similarly *Edomites* is emended from the Hebrew for
'man' = mankind. *Leummim:* this is assumed to be an Arabian
tribe (Gen. 25: 3), but here may simply mean 'peoples' or
'nations'. Precise translation may be difficult but the general
meaning is clear. Because of his love for his people God is
willing to go to any lengths to rescue them.   ✲

WITNESS TO THE UNIQUENESS OF ISRAEL'S GOD

5   Have no fear; for I am with you;
    I will bring your children from the east
     and gather you all from the west.
6   I will say to the north, 'Give them up',
     and to the south, 'Do not hold them back.
   Bring my sons and daughters from afar,
     bring them from the ends of the earth;
7   bring every one who is called by my name,
     all whom I have created, whom I have formed,
   all whom I have made for my glory.'
8   Bring out this people,
     a people who have eyes but are blind,
   who have ears but are deaf.
9   All the nations are gathered together
     and the peoples assembled.
   Who amongst them can expound this thing
     and interpret for us all that has gone before?
   Let them produce witnesses to prove their case,
   or let them listen and say, 'That is the truth.'
10   My witnesses, says the LORD, are you, my servants,
     you whom I have chosen
   to know me and put your faith in me
   and understand that I am He.

Before me there was no god fashioned
nor ever shall be after me.
I am the LORD, I myself,   11
and none but I can deliver.
I myself have made it known in full, and declared it, 12
I and no alien god amongst you,
and you are my witnesses, says the LORD.
I am God; from this very day I am He.   13
What my hand holds, none can snatch away;
what I do, none can undo.

* After a brief introduction recalling the theme of deliverance
from exile the trial scene is renewed. The hitherto blind and
deaf are to be God's witnesses before the nations that the
LORD alone is God; for their history, as it has been interpreted
to them by the prophets, enables them to understand the
meaning of what is now happening. It was for this purpose
that Israel was chosen and created as a people, not for its own
glory but to direct the nations to see the manifest work of
God.

5. The language, if taken literally, suggests a very wide
dispersion of the exiles. But it may be simply a vivid way of
saying 'wherever they are'.

6. *my sons and daughters* alludes to Exod. 4: 22–3 and expresses the strongly personal relationship of God and his
people.

7. *for my glory:* that is, to be the visible manifestation of
God's presence.

8 (cp. 42: 18–20). The reference must be to Israel. The
Hebrew could be read as 'a blind people who (still) have eyes,
deaf but (still) have ears' or 'they have been blind and deaf
but still have the capacity to understand'.

9. The nations are now assembled to hear the evidence
which can in fact be given only from Israel. The prophet

sees this gathering as a certainty for which the Hebrew perfect tense is the one suitable. *amongst them:* Babylonian gods.

10. *my servants:* the Hebrew is singular, 'my servant'. Before the assembled nations Israel is *My witnesses*.

11. *I am the LORD, I myself:* the force of the Hebrew is difficult to render into English, literally 'I, I, Yahweh', recalling the revelation at Sinai, the character of him who is Saviour, and man's response in the age-long prayers and praises offered to him alone. The solemn opening words are picked up in the emphatic repetition of the personal pronoun at the beginning of verses 12 and 13. Israel is recalled to the foundation of its faith and experience, which makes both possible and necessary the function of witnessing. The emphasis is upon what God has done; this makes it possible for men to know him.

12. After *made it known in full*, the Hebrew text has 'and have delivered'; the N.E.B. omits this since it disturbs the poetic structure and may have been accidentally repeated from the end of verse 11. ✶

THE NEW EXODUS

14 Thus says the LORD your ransomer, the Holy One of
   Israel:
 For your sakes I have sent to Babylon;
 I will lay the Chaldaeans prostrate as they flee,
 and their cry of triumph will turn to groaning.
15 I am the LORD, your Holy One,
  your creator, Israel, and your King.

16 Thus says the LORD,
 who opened a way in the sea
 and a path through mighty waters,
17 who drew on chariot and horse to their destruction,

a whole army, men of valour;
 there they lay, never to rise again;
they were crushed, snuffed out like a wick:
  Cease to dwell on days gone by   18
  and to brood over past history.

  Here and now I will do a new thing;   19
   this moment it will break from the bud.
   Can you not perceive it?
I will make a way even through the wilderness
   and paths^{*a*} in the barren desert;
   the wild beasts shall do me honour,   20
   the wolf and the ostrich;
  for I will provide water in the wilderness
   and rivers in the barren desert,
   where my chosen people may drink.
  I have formed this people for myself   21
   and they shall proclaim my praises.

  Yet you did not call upon me, O Jacob; 22
much less did you weary yourself in my service, O
   Israel.
  You did not bring me sheep as whole-offerings 23
   or honour me with sacrifices;
   I asked you for no burdensome offerings
   and wearied you with no demands for incense.
You did not buy me sweet-cane with your money 24
  or glut me with the fat of your sacrifices;
  rather you burdened me with your sins
   and wearied me with your iniquities.
  I alone, I am He,   25
who for his own sake wipes out your transgressions,

[a] *So Scroll; Heb.* rivers.

who will remember your sins no more.[a]
26 Cite me by name, let us argue it out;
set forth your pleading and justify yourselves.
27 Your first father transgressed,
your spokesmen rebelled against me,
28 and your princes profaned my sanctuary;[b]
so I sent Jacob to his doom[c]
and left Israel to execration.

✻ The liberation from exile will be an unprecedented wonder, surpassing even the deliverance from Egypt. In spite of past unfaithfulness Israel will at last learn the fulness of God's forgiveness.

14–15. These verses interrupt the sequence of thought between verses 13 and 16, and may be an independent oracle. But they can be read as a deliberate break, as the more general statements in verses 5–13 and 16–25 are given their particular application in the fall of Babylon. It is this practical application that gives point to what precedes and follows.

Chaldaeans: the first occurrence of this name in these chapters, though frequent in Jeremiah. Chaldaea was a district south-east of Babylonia, but Nabopolassar, the founder of the new Babylonian Empire, was a Chaldaean. Later in the Old Testament period (Daniel) the name became synonymous with astrologers. All translations require some modification of the Hebrew text. The general meaning, the downfall of Babylon, is clear.

16–17 quote from some ancient hymn referring to the exodus from Egypt, in order to prepare the mind for the new divine wonders.

[*a*] remember...no more: *so Scroll; Heb.* not remember your sins.
[*b*] your princes...sanctuary: *prob. rdg., cp. Sept.; Heb.* I have profaned holy princes.
[*c*] sent...doom: *lit.* put Jacob under solemn ban.

18. *Cease to dwell:* literally 'do not remember' but meaning 'do not think only' or 'do not recall nostalgically' (cp. 63: 11–14). In other words the 'good times' were not only in the past but in the present and immediate future. God saved, saves, and will save. This is no time for lamentation but for preparation.

19–20. The theme of the transformation of the desert from a place of death to a place of life occurs in 41: 18f. and also in ch. 35.

21. The function of Israel is to declare in its hymns of worship the saving works of God.

22–4. The demonstration of God's work of salvation itself exposes Israel's infidelity in the past. Too often their worship had been to alien deities, too often their sacrifices were accompanied by lives of wrong-doing. Here the prophet echoes the language of his predecessor in Isa. 1: 11–17. Yet during the exile itself, when sacrifice was no longer possible but obedience was, moral obedience and loyalty were what the LORD required. *wearied* represents a deliberate play on the word 'to serve in worship' or 'to serve with hard work'. Israel by its unworthy worship has made God into a servant.

25. *I alone, I am He:* a recall of the word of revelation. This is at once followed by the definition; *He* is the one who forgives. *for his own sake:* not because Israel deserved it, or has earned it, but because that is what God is like, 'whose nature it is always to forgive'.

26. The final stage in the trial. God has stated his 'case'. What is Israel's defence?

27–8. Beginning with Jacob (Hos. 12: 3) and thereafter, Israel has rebelled. *spokesmen:* apparently false prophets. *princes:* perhaps the kings as high priests. ✻

THE BLESSING OF THE SERVANT

Hear me now, Jacob my servant,   **44**
  hear me, my chosen Israel.

2   Thus says the LORD your maker,
           your helper, who fashioned you from birth:
       have no fear, Jacob my servant,
       Jeshurun whom I have chosen,

3   for I will pour down rain on a thirsty land,
               showers on the dry ground.
       I will pour out my spirit on your offspring
           and my blessing on your children.

4   They shall spring up like[a] a green tamarisk,
           like poplars by a flowing stream.

5   This man shall say, 'I am the LORD's man',
           that one shall call himself a son of Jacob,
       another shall write the LORD's name on his hand
           and shall add the name of Israel to his own.

* This is an oracle of salvation, but with a difference. It declares not what the exiles will be saved from, but what they will be saved for. In fulfilment of the divine choice, they will become numerous, and men of other nations will join them in the worship of the LORD.

1–2. *Hear me now*: the Hebrew 'But now, hear' (cp. 43: 1) emphatically links this with what has preceded, and contrasts the future with the past. Yet this future is a fulfilment of the divine purpose in the very beginning of Israel's life. The unusual name *Jeshurun*, which occurs elsewhere only in Deut. 32: 15; 33: 5, 26, is especially significant. It is an ancient title for Israel whose exact meaning is uncertain but possibly connected with the word for 'upright'. The passage in Deut. 33: 26–9 would be particularly appropriate as an allusion. *have no fear*: cp. 43: 1, 5.

3–4. *rain on a thirsty land* is not, as in 43: 2a, a reference to the march through the desert but a metaphor for the restored

[a] *like: so many MSS.; others* in.

56

Israel. So, *my spirit* means 'my revitalizing power' as in Ezek.
37: 1–14.

5. This is the beginning of a universalism which is developed
more fully and explicitly in subsequent oracles. In one sense
it may be seen as a continuation of what had happened in the
early history of Israel, when many of non-Israelite stock
became Israel through their acknowledgement of Israel's
God (cp. Josh. 9). But that was in the days of a vigorous and
triumphant Israel. Now they were a humiliated people for
whom such an accession of foreigners must have seemed most
improbable. Moreover, the accession of non-Israelites is not
due to the imposition of the religion of a victorious nation,
but the coming into Israel of individuals by deliberate choice. *

THE LORD, HE ALONE, IS GOD

Thus says the LORD, Israel's King,   6
the LORD of Hosts, his ransomer:
I am the first and I am the last,
     and there is no god but me.
Who is like me? Let him stand up,*a*   7
let him declare himself and speak and show me his
          evidence,
let him announce beforehand*b* things to come,
let him*c* declare what is yet to happen.
Take heart, do not be afraid.*d*   8
Did I not foretell this long ago?
I declared it, and you are my witnesses.
Is there any god beside me,
     or any creator, even one that I do not know?

[a] Let him stand up: *so Sept.; Heb. om.*
[b] let him announce beforehand: *prob. rdg.; Heb.* since my appointing
an ancient people and...
[c] *Prob. rdg.; Heb.* them.   [d] be afraid: *so Scroll; Heb.* be foolish.

9   Those who make idols are less than nothing;
        all their cherished images profit nobody;
      their worshippers are blind,
          sheer ignorance makes fools of them.
10 If a man makes a god or casts an image,
        his labour is wasted.
11 Why! its votaries show their folly;
        the craftsmen too are but men.
      Let them all gather together and confront me,
        all will be afraid and look the fools they are.

12 The blacksmith sharpens[a] a graving tool and hammers
    out his work[b] hot from the coals and shapes it with his
    strong arm; when he grows hungry his strength fails,
13 if he has no water to drink he tires. The woodworker
    draws his line taut and marks out a figure with a scriber;
    he planes the wood and measures it with callipers, and
    he carves it to the shape of a man, comely as the human
    form, to be set up presently in a house.
14 A man plants a cedar[d] and the rain makes it grow, so
    that later on he will have cedars to cut down; or he chooses
    an ilex or an oak to raise a stout tree for himself in the
15 forest. It becomes fuel for his fire: some of it he takes and
    warms himself, some he kindles and bakes bread on it,
    and some he makes into a god and prostrates himself,
16 shaping it into an idol and bowing down before it. The
    one half of it he burns in the fire and on this he roasts
    meat, so that he may eat his roast and be satisfied; he also
    warms himself at it and he says, 'Good! I can feel the heat,

[a] sharpens: *so Sept.; Heb. om.*
[b] his work: *prob. rdg.; Heb.* he works.
[c] *Or* a shrine.   [d] *So some MSS.; others* ash-tree.

58

I am growing warm.' Then what is left of the wood he 17
makes into a god by carving it into shape; he bows
down to it and prostrates himself and prays to it, saying,
'Save me; for thou art my god.' Such people neither know 18
nor understand, their eyes made too blind to see, their
minds too narrow to discern. Such a man will not use 19
his reason, he has neither the wit nor the sense to say,
'Half of it I have burnt, yes, and used its embers to bake
bread; I have roasted meat on them too and eaten it;
but the rest of it I turn into this abominable thing and so
I am worshipping a log of wood.'*a* He feeds on ashes 20
indeed! His own deluded mind has misled him, he cannot
recollect himself so far as to say, 'Why! this thing in
my hand is a sham.'

> Remember all this, Jacob,   21
> remember, Israel, for you are my servant,
> I have fashioned you, and you are to serve me;
>   you shall not forget me, Israel.
> I have swept away your sins like a dissolving mist, 22
>   and your transgressions are dispersed like clouds;
> turn back to me; for I have ransomed you.
> Shout in triumph, you heavens, for it is the LORD's doing; 23
>   cry out for joy, you lowest depths of the earth;
> break into songs of triumph, you mountains,
> you forest and all your trees;
> for the LORD has ransomed Jacob
>   and made Israel his masterpiece.

* These verses may be divided into three sections: 6–8, 9–20,
21–3. Of these, verses 21–3 seem to be an appropriate conclu-

[a] a log of wood: *or, with Scroll,* dead wood.

sion to verses 6–8. Verses 9–20 interrupt the sequence of thought with a brilliant satire on the making of idols, and most, if not all, is in prose. The simplest solution is to regard 6–8, 21–3 as a continuous poem, recapitulating themes that have appeared in earlier trial speeches, continuing into an assurance of divine forgiveness and concluding with a hymn of praise. The middle section begins with a taunt-song (verses 9–11) and develops into a sustained satire in prose. While there are no adequate grounds for denying the originality of this section, for we have already noted a similar attitude in 40: 19f.; 41: 6f., it is not easy to see why it was inserted here. Perhaps it was the emphasis on the sole sovereignty of Israel's King in verses 6–8 that caused this section to be included here.

6–8. The oracle opens with a reaffirmation of the majesty of God who acts on behalf of his oppressed people (*ransomer*). He is unique and none can dispute his control of history. The gods of Babylon had failed to prepare their people for the threatened invasion. But the LORD has warned his people and they can meet portentous events without fear, for he can be trusted.

6. *first...last:* the totality of existence finds its origin in him; cp. 'Alpha' and 'Omega', Rev. 1: 8 etc.

8. *creator:* the Hebrew word usually means 'rock' but the N.E.B. here connects it with a similar verb meaning 'to fashion'.

This poem continues in verses 21–3 and notes on these verses will be found below.

9–20. The satire against those who make idols is introduced by a short poetic oracle (verses 9–11) while the remainder is in prose. It may be possible to detect an original poem in verses 12–20 but if so it has been amplified. The argument is clear and related to the historical situation. The great idols of the Babylonian gods were the objects of popular veneration. It is true that the more thoughtful would see them as representations rather than the gods themselves yet, even so, worship and prayer were offered before the idols, and through the idols the gods were believed to hear and respond. It is doubtful whether the prophet was immediately concerned with the beliefs and practices of Babylonian religion except in so far as they affected his fellow Jews. It is all too probable that many of the exiles were in danger of being seduced by the magnificence of Babylonian religion, all the more so in that Israel's God was apparently indifferent to his people's fate, or, at worst, impotent. Moreover, as Ezekiel tells us, popular religion among the Judaeans was not free from idols, in spite of the second commandment. Whatever therefore the general application, this paragraph may be seen as directed towards the Jewish exiles.

Idols, for all the artistic skill, painstaking craftsmanship, and religious devotion offered to them, are the works of man. The materials of which they are made are no different from those which are used for domestic purposes. How can they become objects of veneration? Use your intelligence!

9. *their worshippers:* literally 'their witnesses', which is perhaps more accurate. It is a word of scorn because in fact these gods do nothing that men can witness.

10. *god:* the Hebrew word is not *'elohim* but one that closely corresponds to the Babylonian word for god, i.e. *'El* (cp. 40: 18; 42: 5). The Hebrew sentence is in the form of a question: 'Who can fashion a god?' At once one recalls Gen. 2: 7 where the same verb is used of the shaping of man from dust!

12–13. A number of rare words occur in this passage, apparently technical terms. *scriber* is something like a carpenter's pencil. *house:* probably 'shrine', as in the footnote, would be better.

15–17. A good example of the fact that genuine religion generates rational thinking. How can you really worship a god whose image is made from what is left over from firewood?

18 is a comment perhaps drawn from wisdom teaching.

19. *abominable thing:* i.e. that which is religiously or ritually offensive.

20. *he cannot recollect himself:* or, more literally, 'he will not save his life'. This verse is no longer satire, but the prophet's own estimate of what he has described.

21–3. These verses conclude the poem begun in verses 6–8. If we see verses 6–8 as recapitulation, 'all this' (literally 'these') is appropriate, and leads to the conclusion in verses 21f. The character of God has been summarily stated: now the role of Israel is briefly stated in that setting.

21. *Remember, Israel:* this is based on a slight emendation of the Masoretic Text supported by the Septuagint and the Dead Sea Scroll.

23 is a final burst of praise, bringing this whole section to a close; cp. 42: 10–13. *made Israel his masterpiece* is a somewhat free rendering of the Hebrew, literally 'will glorify himself in Israel', i.e. the redeemed Israel is the visible expression of God's glory. The same word is used in 49: 3: 'through whom I shall win glory'. *

CYRUS AS GOD'S ANOINTED KING

24   Thus says the LORD, your ransomer,
         who fashioned you from birth:
     I am the LORD who made all things,
         by myself I stretched out the skies,
         alone I hammered out the floor of the earth.

25   I frustrate false prophets and their signs
         and make fools of diviners;
     I reverse what wise men say
         and make nonsense of their wisdom.

26   I make my servants' prophecies come true
         and give effect to my messengers' designs.
     I say of Jerusalem,

'She shall be inhabited once more',
  and of the cities of Judah, 'They shall be rebuilt;
    all their ruins I will restore.'
I say to the deep waters, 'Be dried up;   27
  I will make your streams run dry.'
I say to Cyrus, 'You shall be my shepherd   28
  to carry out all my purpose,
so that Jerusalem may be rebuilt
  and the foundations of the temple may be
    laid.'[a]

Thus says the LORD to Cyrus his anointed,   **45**
  Cyrus whom he has taken by the hand
  to subdue nations before him
  and undo the might[b] of kings;
  before whom gates shall be opened
    and no doors be shut:
I will go before you   2
  and level the swelling hills;
  I will break down gates of bronze
  and hack through iron bars.
I will give you treasures from dark vaults,   3
  hoarded in secret places,
that you may know that I am the LORD,
  Israel's God who calls you by name.
For the sake of Jacob my servant and Israel my chosen 4
  I have called you by name
and given you your title, though you have not known
    me.

[a] may be laid: *prob. rdg., cp. Scroll; Heb.* you may be laid.
[b] might: *lit.* loins.

5   I am the LORD, there is no other;
        there is no god beside me.
        I will strengthen you though you have not known
            me,
6   so that men from the rising and the setting sun
        may know that there is none but I:
        I am the LORD, there is no other;
7   I make the light, I create darkness,
            author alike of prosperity and trouble.
    I, the LORD, do all these things.

8   Rain righteousness, you heavens,
        let the skies above pour down;
            let the earth open to receive it,
                that it may bear the fruit of salvation
    with righteousness in blossom at its side.
    All this I, the LORD, have created.

✻ This passage contains two parts of one poem, 44: 24–8 and 45: 1–7 and ends with a brief hymn, 45: 8. The first part is a careful preparation for the astonishing statement that Cyrus, the pagan king, is to be God's choice of one who shall inherit the role and functions of the Davidic king (cp. Ps. 2). These words must have come as a profound shock to the hearers; perhaps the series of phrases describing God's acts in creation and history indicate the mental struggle of the prophet himself as he receives the word of the LORD. Verses 24–8 contain a whole series of participles in Hebrew which could be represented in English by relative clauses, as in the Revised Standard Version. It is as though the prophet is made to recall all that he has said about God in order that he may be able to accept the oracle 'I say to Cyrus "You shall be my shepherd"', and then to receive the oracle 'to Cyrus his anointed'.

24. *I am the LORD:* nothing less than this solemn affirmation can justify the statements in 44: 28; 45: 1.

25. *false prophets:* literally 'babblers', 'boasters', but the N.E.B. may be emending the word to correspond to a guild of Babylonian prophets. *wise men:* the Babylonian king's counsellors.

26. *servants' prophecies:* Hebrew has 'the word of his servant' which would seem to mean 'the revelation entrusted to Israel'. The N.E.B. represents a small emendation which is widely accepted.

27. *deep waters:* the Hebrew word occurs only here, and appears to refer to the waters of the abyss around and under the earth.

28. *shepherd* is a regular title of the king in the ancient world; thus Hammurabi, king of Babylon, describes himself as 'the shepherd that brings good' (cp. also 2 Sam. 5: 2). But the pronoun *my* emphasizes that he has been appointed by the LORD to rule Israel. (The closing two lines of this verse are, in Hebrew, awkwardly expressed, and partly repeat words in verse 26. They may be due to a later commentator and were then transferred from the margin to the text.)

45: 1. *his anointed:* this is a distinctively Israelite title, in the monarchy period almost exclusively used of kings. It is the Hebrew *mashiaḥ* (hence *messiah* and Greek *Christos*). Only here is it used of one who is not a member of the covenant community. Although the ascription had not acquired the messianic associations of a later age, it is startling enough. Two implications are clear: (1) From the Jewish point of view Cyrus is to fulfil the hopes centred on the Davidic king (see e.g. Ps. 72). (2) It is not the conqueror's god, but the LORD, God of Israel, who has appointed Cyrus as king. The clauses in this verse after *anointed* are in the first person singular: 'I have taken', 'I will undo'; and are spoken about Cyrus. They appear to be in the first instance an oracle to the prophet. *by the hand:* in the Cyrus Cylinder Cyrus speaks of Marduk taking his hand, i.e. making him ruler.

2. This is the beginning of the oracle to Cyrus and continues to verse 7. The language of verses 2–5 is taken from the ritual of coronation.

3. *calls you by name:* this may refer to the giving of an accession name as in Isa. 9: 6, but it also refers to God's exercise of authority over Cyrus. *that you may know:* the prophet recognizes that Cyrus may be ignorant of Israel's God (verses 4 and 5), but Cyrus will learn who has given him the victory.

4. The divine purpose in choosing Cyrus is for the deliverance of Israel, in order that this people may fulfil their destined role.

6. The ultimate divine purpose in choosing Cyrus is that all the world may know the LORD.

7. *prosperity and trouble:* the words cover the whole range of what is good and evil, and must not be given a narrowly moral meaning. Here the N.E.B. gives the English equivalent. So also in Amos 3: 6 'disaster' renders the same word as 'trouble'.

8. The brief hymn of triumph brings this section on Cyrus to its conclusion. *righteousness* includes the victory of God's righteous purpose; cp. Ps. 85: 10–13. ✶

AGAINST THE CRITICS

9   Will the pot contend[a] with the potter,
      or the earthenware[b] with the hand that shapes it?
    Will the clay ask the potter what he is making?
      or his[c] handiwork say to him, 'You have no skill'?
10   Will the babe say[d] to his father, 'What are you begetting?',
      or to his mother, 'What are you bringing to birth?'

[a] Will...contend: *prob. rdg.; Heb.* Ho! he has contended.
[b] *Or* shard.
[c] *Prob. rdg.; Heb.* your.
[d] Will...say: *prob. rdg.; Heb.* Ho! you that say.

Thus says the LORD, Israel's Holy One, his maker: 11
　Would you dare question me concerning my
　　children,
　or instruct me in my handiwork?
　I alone, I made the earth   12
　and created man upon it;
I, with my own hands, stretched out the heavens
　and caused all their host to shine.
　I alone have roused this man in righteousness,   13
　　and I will smooth his path before him;
　he shall rebuild my city
　　and let my exiles go free –
　　not for a price nor for a bribe,
　　says the LORD of Hosts.

✶ It is not surprising that the prophet's message met with a mixed reception. Many would wish to believe in his message of salvation, but found it impossible. When he used this precise language about the pagan king, that he was the LORD's anointed king – language that could properly be used only of the Davidic dynasty – this was not only incredible but offensive. Cyrus was certainly not a descendant of David (cp. 2 Sam. 8: 16) and was not an Israelite (cp. Deut. 17: 15), and was not a worshipper of the LORD, as the prophet himself had said (45: 4f.). To this the prophet's reply is: it is not for man to question the sovereign purpose of God in his work of salvation. This is not, of course, an argument. It will convince only those who share the prophet's faith. But that is precisely what his hearers should have shared.

9. The metaphor of the *potter* with his *clay* is a natural one to emphasize the absolute sovereignty of God, especially since the word for *potter* is the same verb that is translated 'formed' in Gen. 2: 7. It may be noted (see the N.E.B. footnotes *a* and *d*) that the Masoretic Text begins verses 9

and 10 with an exclamation of grief, implying here also reproach. The Dead Sea Scroll has the same exclamation also in the second half of verse 9.

10. If verse 9 reproaches those who would impugn the sovereignty of God, this verse describes this as grave impropriety in terms of the family.

13. *in righteousness:* the meaning is 'for my triumphant purpose'. *not for a price:* formally this seems to contradict 43: 3, but the prophet there is insisting that the lands and people are completely at God's disposal, and, in this verse, so is the world conqueror. ✻

THE NATIONS FIND GOD IN ISRAEL

14   Thus says the LORD:
        Toilers of Egypt and Nubian merchants
        and Sabaeans bearing tribute*a*
    shall come into your power and be your slaves,
    shall come and march behind you in chains;
    they shall bow down before you in supplication, saying,
    'Surely God is among you and there is no other,
        no other god.
15   How then canst thou be a god that hidest thyself,
        O God of Israel, the deliverer?'

16   Those who defy him*b* are confounded and brought to
            shame,
    those who make idols perish in confusion.
17   But Israel has been delivered by the LORD,
        delivered for all time to come;
    they shall not be confounded or put to shame for all
            eternity.

[a] bearing tribute: *or* men of stature.
[b] Those who defy him: *so Sept.; Heb.* All of them together.

Thus says the LORD, the creator of the heavens, 18
    he who is God,
  who made the earth and fashioned it
    and himself fixed it fast,
  who created it no empty void,
    but made it for a place to dwell in:
  I am the LORD, there is no other.
I do not speak in secret, in realms of darkness, 19
  I do not say to the sons of Jacob,
    'Look for me in the empty void.'
I the LORD speak what is right, declare what is
        just.
  Gather together, come, draw near, 20
    all you survivors of the nations,
  you fools, who carry your wooden idols in procession
  and pray to a god that cannot save you.
Come forward and urge your case, consult[a] together: 21
  who foretold this in days of old,
    who stated it long ago?
  Was it not I the LORD?
  There is no god but me;
there is no god other than I, victorious and able to save.
  Look to me and be saved, 22
    you peoples from all corners of the earth;
  for I am God, there is no other.
  By my life I have sworn, 23
I have given a promise of victory,
    a promise that will not be broken,
that to me every knee shall bend
    and by me every tongue shall swear.

[a] *So Vulg.; Heb.* let them consult.

24   In the LORD alone, men shall say,
          are victory and might;
      and all who defy him
      shall stand ashamed in his presence,
25   but all the sons of Israel shall stand victorious
          and find their glory in the LORD.

✶ The magnificence and daring of the prophetic faith is
unmistakable. It is claimed that the God, Yahweh, of this
defeated and humiliated people is about to be acknowledged
as the one true God by all mankind and that in him alone is
salvation. But this is not simply the faith of the prophet; it
is the word of revelation, 'Thus says the LORD' (verses 14 and
18). These two oracles are separated by a reflection by the
prophet (verses 16f.).

14. Who is being addressed? Since the pronouns *your, you*
are feminine singular, the reference appears to be to Zion
representing Israel, the worshipping community (cp. 40: 2, 9).
The nations of the Nile valley (cp. 43: 3) represent the further-
most people. *bearing tribute:* the word translated 'tribute'
occurs again in Neh. 5: 4 as 'money'. But the whole passage
is more usually translated 'men of stature' (cp. the N.E.B.
footnote *a*) as in Num. 13: 32: 'men of gigantic size'. The footnote translation would be appropriate as in Isa. 18: 2, 7
although a different word is used for 'tall'. *shall come into
your power and be your slaves* is more precise than the Hebrew
requires; literally it is, 'shall come over to you and be yours'
(Revised Standard Version). The English phrase 'belong to
you' is similarly ambiguous and could mean that these people
will become part of the new Israel by conversion. *in chains*
could then be understood as captives, in a metaphorical sense,
in the light of the portrait of God as the victorious King (40:
10; 44: 6). It is doubtful whether the prophet thought of
the heathen nations as literally slaves and captives of Israel.
Similarly, it is improbable that the prophet meant that the

heathen were to bow down and pray to Israel, except in the
sense that the worshipping Israel was the temple of the living
God. This leads to the confession at the end of the verse introduced by *Surely* for which the Hebrew word conveys the
meaning 'contrary to all that we thought'.

15. Literally, 'Truly thou art a God who hidest thyself.'
Again the first word emphasizes the unexpected. It is the
incredible truth that the reality of God is to be found among
this humiliated and insignificant people. The God whom men
seek is the God of Israel. This may be regarded as the Old
Testament equivalent of Phil. 2: 6-11 where in fact Isa. 45: 23
is quoted.

16-17. These two verses, a reflective word of the prophet,
relieve the dramatic tension induced by the climax of verses
14-15. He contrasts the *confusion* of those who make idols
with the experience of salvation in Israel.

18. A further word of the LORD using the language of
hymns. It is Yahweh, God of Israel, who created the ordered
world from the primaeval chaos (cp. Gen. 1: 2).

19. *in secret:* the noun picks up the verb in verse 15 'hidest
thyself'. The word of God has been clearly spoken in his
proclamation of what is *right* and *just. realms of darkness* may
refer to She'ol, the place of the dead, and therefore allude to
the practice of necromancy.

20-1. The familiar language of the trial. The *survivors of
the nations* appears to describe immediately those who,
trusting in their impotent gods, collapsed before the divinely
given power of Cyrus. *idols in procession* refers to the practice
of the New Year Festival, the supreme occasion in the
Babylonian religion. *days of old* and *long ago:* the work of
Israel's prophets and the language of the enthronement
psalms (cp. Pss. 2: 8-12; 110: 1-2) are referred to. Note the
equation of the words *victorious* ('righteous') and *able to save*
('saviour').

22-4. The *victory* (righteous acts) and *might* of God lie in
his royal summons to all men individually to receive his

salvation and to worship him. *By my life*, literally 'by myself',
is the most solemn form of the oath (by Yahweh) put into
the mouth of God. *a promise* (word) is the effective word
which nothing can annul or hinder (cp. 43: 13).

25. The one-time heathen will participate in singing their
hallelujahs (*find their glory*). ✳

IMPOTENT GODS AND THE GOD OF MIGHT

46   Bel has crouched down, Nebo has stooped low:
their images, once carried in your processions,
    have been loaded on to beasts and cattle,
    a burden for the weary creatures;
2   they stoop and they crouch;
not for them to bring the burden to safety;
    the gods themselves go into captivity.

3   Listen to me, house of Jacob
    and all the remnant of the house of Israel,
a load on me from your birth, carried by me from the
        womb:
4   till you grow old I am He,
    and when white hairs come, I will carry you still;
I have made you and I will bear the burden,
    I will carry you and bring you to safety.

5   To whom will you liken me? Who is my equal?
    With whom can you compare me? Where is my like?

6   Those who squander their bags of gold
    and weigh out their silver with a balance
hire a goldsmith to fashion them into a god;
    then they worship it and fall prostrate before it;
7   they hoist it shoulder-high and carry it home;
      they set it down on its base;

there it must stand, it cannot stir from its place.
Let a man cry to it as he will, it never answers him;
    it cannot deliver him from his troubles.

Remember this, you rebels,   8
consider it well, and abandon hope,
remember all that happened long ago;   9
for I am God, there is no other,
I am God, and there is no one like me;
I reveal the end from the beginning,   10
from ancient times I reveal what is to be;
I say, 'My purpose shall take effect,
I will accomplish all that I please.'
I summon a bird of prey[a] from the east,   11
one from a distant land to fulfil my purpose.
    Mark this; I have spoken, and I will bring it
        about,
I have a plan to carry out, and carry it out I will.
Listen to me, all you stubborn hearts,   12
    for whom victory is far off:
I bring my victory near, it is not far off,   13
    and my deliverance shall not be delayed;
I will grant deliverance in Zion
    and give my glory to Israel.[b]

✶ The great vision of ch. 45 is now directed to a particular
situation, that of Babylon, where the mighty gods of the
empire were worshipped with magnificent ceremonial. But
it was all an empty show. These gods were in fact impotent
in the very situation in which they must, if they are gods,

[a] a bird of prey: *or* a massed host.
[b] and give my glory to Israel: *or* for Israel my glory.

come to the help of their devotees. Worse, they were an added burden to those whose burdens they should have relieved; can they really be gods?

The words are primarily to the exiles (verse 3), many of whom were in danger of being seduced by the apparent superiority of Babylon's gods, and by the magnificent spectacles of Babylon's rituals. Now they will see for themselves how futile these gods are, and return in penitence and renewed confidence to the incomparable LORD who through his prophet has foretold the downfall of Babylon and will assuredly deliver his people. Note the imperatives in verses 3, 8, 9 and 12.

1. *Bel* is similar to the Hebrew *ba'al*, originally the father of the gods, with whom Marduk was identified, whose temple was the chief shrine in Babylon; *Nebo* or Nabu, son of Marduk, keeper of the tablets of destiny and therefore the god of prophecy; these were the gods who were believed to have given Babylon the empire of the world. In the New Year Festival, their images were carried in solemn procession from their temples to the Euphrates and returned with spectacular rituals. But now they are an encumbrance for a people, fleeing from the oncoming armies of Cyrus, who must rescue the gods who should have protected them! Perhaps the divine names are particularly significant since the Babylonian king was named Nabonidus, and his son and co-regent was Bel-shar-uṣur ('Nabu is awe-inspiring' and 'Bel protect the king').

2. *the gods themselves go into captivity:* in this brief sentence the futility of the gods is exposed. It should be noted that this prophecy was not literally fulfilled. Babylon in fact capitulated before Cyrus, and Cyrus claimed the support of the Babylonian gods for the conquest of the empire. But this does not invalidate the argument. Her gods were unable to save the empire.

3–4. By contrast, the LORD is the burden-bearer, Israel is the burden. Was this passage in the mind of Jesus in Matt. 11: 28?

5–7. After the climax of verse 4, this is a parenthesis before the concluding oracle of salvation. It does not so much break the continuity between verses 4 and 8, as pause for a moment of reflection. The gods of Babylon are as incapable of action and response to prayer as the images which represent them (cp. 45: 20).

8. *Remember* includes the idea of acting appropriately. *rebels* refers to those exiles who were forsaking the living God for the gods of Babylon. They should remember the long history of salvation and prophetic interpretation of history.

11. *bird of prey* refers to Cyrus whose original kingdom was north-east of Babylon. N.E.B. footnote *a* 'a massed host' would refer to the armies led by Cyrus. *Mark this:* the Hebrew interjection, to which this corresponds, occurs three times in this sentence. It emphasizes the absolute certainty of the fulfilment of the divine purpose in history.

12–13. *victory:* i.e. the triumph of God's righteous purpose. Because the exiles are *stubborn* this triumph seems remote, but in fact it is at hand. Then the divine majesty and rule will be manifest in all the worshipping community and will reach out to all mankind. ✳

THE COLLAPSE OF BABYLON

Down with you, sit in the dust,   **47**
  virgin daughter of Babylon.
Down from your throne, sit on the ground,
  daughter of the Chaldaeans;
never again shall men call you
  soft-skinned and delicate.
Take up the millstone, grind meal, uncover your ₂
  tresses;
strip off your skirt, bare your thighs, wade through
  rivers,

3   so that your nakedness may be plain to see
          and your shame exposed.
   I will take vengeance, I will treat with none of you,
4   says[a] the Holy One of Israel, our ransomer,
          whose name is the LORD of Hosts.

5   Sit silent,
       be off into the shadows, daughter of the Chaldaeans;
       for never again shall men call you
          queen of many kingdoms.
6   When I was angry with my people,
       I dishonoured my own possession
          and gave them into your power.
       You showed them no mercy,
       you made your yoke weigh heavy on the aged.
7   You said then, 'I shall reign a queen for ever',
          while[b] you gave no thought to this
          and did not consider how it would end.
8   Now therefore listen to this,
       you lover of luxury, carefree on your throne.
          You say to yourself,
       'I am, and who but I?
       No widow's weeds for me, no deaths of children.'
9   Yet suddenly, in a single day,
          these two things shall come upon you;
       they shall both come upon you in full measure:[c]
          children's deaths and widowhood,
          for all your monstrous sorceries, your countless spells.

[a] says: *so Sept.; Heb. om.*
[b] for ever', while: *or* of a wide realm, for all time'; but.
[c] in full measure: *or* at random.

Secure in your wicked ways you thought, 'No one is 10
    looking.'
Your wisdom betrayed you, omniscient as you were,
    and you said to yourself,
'I am, and who but I?'
Therefore evil shall come upon you,   11
    and you will not know how to master it;
disaster shall befall you,
    and you will not be able to charm it away;
    ruin all unforeseen
shall come suddenly upon you.

Persist in your spells and your monstrous sorceries,[a] 12
maybe you can get help from them,
    maybe you will yet inspire awe.
But no! in spite of your many wiles you are   13
    powerless.
Let your astrologers, your star-gazers
who foretell your future month by month,
    persist, and save you!
But look, they are gone like chaff;   14
    fire burns them up;
they cannot snatch themselves from the flames;
    this is no glowing coal to warm them,
no fire for them to sit by.
So much for your magicians   15
with whom you have trafficked all your life:
they have stumbled off, each his own way,
    and there is no one to save you.

[a] *Prob. rdg.; Heb. adds* with which you have trafficked all your life
(*cp. verse 15*).

✻ This is a superb poem, brilliant in its imagery, vigorous in its language. To appreciate its quality it should be read aloud. It is notoriously difficult to render poetry into another language, but the N.E.B. has gone far to convey the spirit of this poem. It may still be useful to read other versions; among recent translations the Revised Standard Version and the Jerusalem Bible will be helpful.

Most of the poem is in the form normally associated with a funeral dirge of which a brief example occurs in Amos 5: 2, and extended examples in Lamentations. The poem should also be compared with Isa. 14: 4–21, although in that poem it is the downfall of Babylon's king that is described. The dirge form indicates the prophet's certainty that this mighty world empire is about to come to an end. The poem contains six strophes. Verses 1–4: Babylon, the centre of the empire, is portrayed as a proud empress surrounded by every luxury, now reduced to the condition of the most menial slave-girl. Verses 5–7: the victorious empress will be cast into a dark dungeon, because, having been given the victory over Israel, she has treated her captives mercilessly. Verses 8–9: confident in her security, she will suddenly find herself bereft and forsaken. Verses 10–11: secure in her self-sufficiency, she will plunge into ruin. Verses 12–13: in spite of their worldwide reputation, Babylon's magicians are unable to save. Verses 14–15: the magicians themselves will be consumed in the irresistible fire, leaving Babylon helpless.

1. *virgin daughter* is frequently used of Jerusalem under attack (cp. Lam. 2: 13), but now of Babylon.

2. *uncover your tresses:* it would be a mark of humiliation for a great lady to go about without a covering for the hair. The Revised Standard Version 'put off your veil' has much the same significance, but the N.E.B. is to be preferred.

3. *I will take vengeance* conveys a false impression in English. It is the action whereby a wronged person is restored to his rights (avenged) or a wrong-doer is properly punished. It is not vindictiveness but vindication.

5. *be off into the shadows:* i.e. 'go to prison'.

6. *dishonoured:* literally 'profaned'. God had ceased to treat Israel as a holy nation and allowed them to be treated as any other nation and so conquered by Babylon. But this did not condone Babylonian ill-treatment of the captives.

8. '*I am, and who but I?*' Cp. verse 10. This is not an assertion of equality with God as the English 'I am' might suggest. The Hebrew text simply has the pronoun 'I'. It is an arrogant assertion of superiority over all other nations, an assertion soon to be falsified.

9. The metaphor of childless widowhood describes the pitiful fate of Babylon that is about to come upon her.

10. '*No one is looking*': cp. Pss. 10: 11; 94: 7. The arrogant 'queen' thinks of herself above the law, like Jezebel in 1 Kings 21: 7–14. Throughout these strophes the frequent mention of magical practices is particularly appropriate to Babylon where such practices were common.

13. *your many wiles* or 'the many words of advice given to you (by your astrologers etc.)'. The belief that human life, national and individual, was governed by the apparent movement of stars and planets was highly developed in Babylonia.

14. The magicians themselves will be consumed in a raging conflagration which they were powerless to predict or avert.

15. *each his own way:* i.e. in panic-stricken flight. ✶

THE PROMISED DELIVERANCE IS AT HAND

Hear this, you house of Jacob,　　　　　**48**
you who are called by the name of Israel,
you who spring from the seed of Judah;
who swear by the name of the LORD
and boast in the God of Israel,
but not in honesty or sincerity,
although you call yourselves citizens of a holy city　₂

and lean for support on the God of Israel;
his name is the LORD of Hosts.

3   Long ago I announced what would first happen,
I revealed it with my own mouth;
suddenly I acted and it came about.

4   I knew that you were stubborn,
your neck stiff as iron, your brow like bronze,

5   therefore I told you of these things long ago,
and declared them before they came about,
so that you could not say, 'This was my idol's
doing;
my image, the god that I fashioned, he ordained
them.'

6   You have heard what I said; consider it well,
and you must admit the truth of it.
Now I show you new things,
hidden things which you did not know before.

7   They were not created long ago, but in this very
hour;
you had never heard of them before today.
You cannot say, 'I know them already.'

8   You neither heard nor knew,
long ago your ears were closed;
for I knew that you were untrustworthy, treacherous,
a notorious rebel from your birth.

9   For the sake of my own name I was patient,[a]
rather than destroy you I held myself in check.

10 See how I tested you, not as silver is tested,
but in the furnace of affliction; there I purified
you.

[a] *See note on verse 11.*

For my honour, for my own honour I did it;   11
let them disparage my past triumphs*a* if they will:
I will not give my glory to any other god.

Hear me, Jacob,   12
    and Israel whom I called:
I am He; I am the first,
    I am the last also.
With my own hands I founded the earth,   13
with my right hand I formed the expanse of sky;
    when I summoned them,
        they sprang at once into being.
Assemble, all of you, and listen to me;   14
    which of you*b* has declared what is coming,
that he whom I*c* love shall wreak my*d* will on Babylon
    and the Chaldaeans shall be scattered?
I, I myself, have spoken, I have called him,   15
I have made him appear, and wherever he goes he shall
        prosper.
Draw near to me and hear this: 16
    from the beginning I have never spoken in secret;
    from the moment of its first happening I was there.*e*

Thus says the LORD your ransomer, the Holy One of   17
    Israel:
    I am the LORD your God:
        I teach you for your own advantage
    and lead you in the way you must go.
    If only you had listened to my commands,   18

[a] my past triumphs: *transposed from verse 9.*
[b] *So many MSS.; others* them.
[c] *Prob. rdg., cp. Sept.; Heb. adds* the LORD.   [d] *Or* his.
[e] *Prob. rdg.; Heb. adds* and now the Lord GOD has sent me, and his spirit.

your prosperity would have rolled on like a river in flood
and your just success like the waves of the sea;
19   in number your children would have been like the
sand
and your descendants countless as its grains;
their name would never be erased or blotted from my
sight.
20   Come out of Babylon, hasten away from the
Chaldaeans;
proclaim it with loud songs of triumph,
crying the news to the ends of the earth;
tell them, 'The LORD has ransomed his servant Jacob.'
21   Though he led them through desert places they suffered
no thirst,
for them he made water run from the rock,
for them he cleft the rock and streams gushed forth.

22   There is no peace for the wicked,
says the LORD.

∗ This chapter forms the climax to what has been said in the preceding chapters. It is addressed to the exiles with some sharpness and a note of urgency as it leads to the summons to leave Babylon. It recapitulates some of the themes in the earlier chapters, and concludes this section of Second Isaiah with a word of triumph which is to resound among the nations. There are difficulties of interpretation in detail, and the sequence of thought is not always clear. Some would see here three or four independent poems, but there is no agreement about the limits of each poem, except the first (verses 1–11). Others would see in this chapter one poem. It may be convenient to adopt the divisions suggested in the N.E.B., verses 1–11, 12–16, 17–21, but to treat the chapter as a unity.

Verse 22 is a separate concluding comment. The argument will then be: verses 1–11 – in spite of Israel's stubbornness, God has made clear his activity in his people's history. Now he is announcing 'new things' so that there can be no misunderstanding about his control of history. Some of the condemnations of Israel in this section are harsher than elsewhere in Second Isaiah (cp. 42: 18–25), particularly as they are addressed to a humiliated people. But the prophet would see Israel as a unity of past, present and future. It is essential for the chastened Israel of the present and Israel moving into its glorious future to recognize itself as one with the disloyal Israel of the past. It may well be that there is a deliberate recall of Ezekiel's words to the exiles (Ezek. 2: 4; 3: 7). Deliverance, which is about to come, must be from a self-inflicted 'exile' from God, as well as from the exile imposed from without. Verses 12–16 – this same God is at work in this new situation to overthrow the Babylonian Empire by the victories of Cyrus, and he has forewarned Israel. Therefore (verses 17–22) Israel must not be disobedient and distrustful as in the past, but 'ransomed, healed, restored, forgiven', receive with joy this mighty act of salvation and proclaim it 'to the ends of the earth'.

1. *Hear:* this verb is one of the keynotes of the chapter. In various forms of the Hebrew verb it occurs seven times. *called* occurs six times. This verse, until the last line, and verse 2, carefully define what is meant by Israel. *swear by:* literally 'remember' or 'confess' (Revised Standard Version).

2. *citizens of a holy city* is less a political phrase than a term meaning 'fellow-citizens with God's people' (Eph. 2: 19). Israel is the people of God at worship.

3–5. What God has foretold through the prophets has come to pass. The fulfilment is a rebuke to the disloyal.

6–8. Now the new act of deliverance is declared as something totally unexpected.

9–11. In spite of the fact that Israel's disloyalty to the Covenant God deserved death, the divine judgement has *purified* his people in order to renew the covenant; thus his *glory*, i.e. his self-manifestation, may be seen in his intervention within history.

12–16. This new act of deliverance effected through Cyrus is set within the context of God's work in creation. The LORD whom they thought to have been defeated is in fact the Creator of the world and the sole ruler of history.

14. *he whom I love* has a striking parallel in the Cyrus Cylinder: 'I am Cyrus...whose rule Bel and Nabu cherish, whose kingship they desire for their heart's pleasure.'

16. This verse is like a signature to a solemn document. The God who is now effecting his purpose through Cyrus is the same as he who worked through Moses and the prophets. The closing line to this verse is given in the footnote as a saying out of context. It can hardly be a gloss since it explains nothing. Its significance is obscure. It may be an isolated word of the prophet to his disciples. 'his spirit' is a second object to 'sent'. A possible meaning could be 'The LORD has sent me, his prophet, to declare these things and his spirit to effect them ', and if this meaning is adopted, then the words provide an apt conclusion to this part of the poem; they underline both the prophet's function and the absolute certainty of God's action.

17–19. This divine admonition to Israel in exile recalls the language of Pss. 81: 13–14; 95: 7. It is an expression of the divine compassion for a people who had so far failed to realize their true destiny, but may yet do so.

18. *prosperity* rightly understands the Hebrew *shalom*. It includes material prosperity but also that condition of the inner life that makes for healthy relationships between man and God, and between man and his neighbour, which makes real prosperity possible. *your just success* means your triumphant realization of God's righteous purpose.

20–1. These verses conclude the poem with a joyful hymn. The prophet is so confident of the victory of God's purpose that he tells his fellow exiles to get ready at once to leave

Babylon before it is overwhelmed; cp. Jer. 51: 6–10. The exiles are to leave singing the triumph song which recapitulates the exodus from Egypt; cp. Exod. 17: 6; Ps. 105: 41. Yet this second exodus is to be more wonderful than the first, since the divine work of salvation is good news for all mankind.

22. This verse is similar to 57: 21, where it is more appropriate. Perhaps it was added here as a final warning in the light of verses 4–11. *peace* is the same word as 'prosperity' in verse 18. With these words the first section of Second Isaiah is concluded. *

Israel a light to the nations

ISRAEL'S FUTURE GLORY

* In chs. 49–55 we have a distinct section in the prophecies of Second Isaiah. The emphasis here is not on the exiled Jews in Babylon, but on Zion–Jerusalem awaiting the return of the exiles, and its rehabilitation. This change of emphasis is so striking that some scholars have suggested that the prophet had left Babylon and was preaching to the depressed Judaeans in Palestine. This may not be necessary, since, as we know from Jeremiah and Ezekiel, the conditions of those in Judaea were well known to those in Babylon. In other words, the prophet, having proclaimed with joyful confidence the release of the Jews from exile, projects his mind to his fellow Jews in the homeland, to prepare them for what he is quite certain will happen. But he is no mere visionary; he knows full well the practical difficulties (most would have said impossibilities) to be overcome. He is equally certain that they will be overcome by God the Creator and Saviour. Ezekiel, too, in his own distinctive way, had also prepared for a new Jerusalem (Ezek. 40–8). *

REASSURANCE

49   Listen to me, you coasts and islands,
      pay heed, you peoples far away:
      from birth the LORD called me,
      he named me from my mother's womb.

2   He made my tongue[a] his sharp sword
      and concealed me under cover of his hand;
      he made me a polished arrow
      and hid me out of sight in his quiver.

3   He said to me, 'You are my servant,
      Israel through whom I shall win glory';
      so I rose to honour in the LORD's sight
      and my God became my strength.[b]

4   Once I said, 'I have laboured in vain;
      I have spent my strength for nothing, to no purpose';
      yet in truth my cause is with the LORD
      and my reward is in God's hands.

5   And now the LORD who formed me in the womb to
      be his servant,
      to bring Jacob back to him
      that Israel should be gathered to him,[c]
      now the LORD calls me again:[d]

6   it is too slight a task for you, as my servant,
      to restore the tribes of Jacob,
      to bring back the descendants of Israel:
      I will make you a light to the nations,
      to be my salvation[e] to earth's farthest bounds.

[a] *Lit.* mouth.   [b] so I rose...strength: *transposed from end of verse 5.*
[c] be gathered to him: *or* not be swept away.   [d] *See note on verse 3.*
[e] to be my salvation: *or* that my salvation may reach.

Thus says the Holy One, the LORD who ransoms 7
       Israel,
   to one who thinks little of himself,*a*
   whom every nation abhors,
   the slave of tyrants:
 When they see you kings shall rise;
 princes shall rise and bow down,
 because of the LORD who is faithful,
because of the Holy One of Israel who has chosen you.

Thus says the LORD: 8
   In the hour of my favour I answered you,
   and I helped you on the day of deliverance,*b*
   putting the land to rights
 and sharing out afresh its desolate fields;
 I said to the prisoners, 'Go free', 9
 and to those in darkness, 'Come out and be seen.'
 They shall find pasture in the desert sands*c*
 and grazing on all the dunes.

   They shall neither hunger nor thirst, 10
 no scorching heat or sun shall distress them;
   for one who loves them shall lead them
   and take them to water at bubbling springs.
 I will make every hill a path 11
   and build embankments for my highways.
 See, they come; some from far away, 12
 these from the north and these from the west
   and those from the land of Syene.*d*

[*a*] to one...himself: *prob. rdg., cp. Sept.; Heb. obscure.*   [*b*] *Prob. rdg.;*
Heb. adds I have formed you, and appointed you to be a light to all
peoples (*cp. 42: 6*).   [*c*] desert sands: *prob. rdg.; Heb.* ways.   [*d*] *So*
Scroll; Heb. Sinim.

13   Shout for joy, you heavens, rejoice, O earth,
           you mountains, break into songs of triumph,
        for the LORD has comforted his people
           and has had pity on his own in their distress.

✳ Ch. 49 begins (verses 1–6) with a poem often numbered as
the second Servant Poem in which the Servant recalls his
commissioning, his apparent failure, his renewal of faith, and
his role as the agent of God's salvation within and beyond
Israel. In a brief parenthesis (verse 7) the humiliated 'slave
of tyrants' is reassured by God's faithfulness. This is then made
explicit first (verses 8–13) by God's care for the exiles
who will be restored from all parts of the world, and then
(verses 14–26) by a vivid picture of a reinhabited Zion. The
main theme of the chapter is clear, although there are difficulties in translation (see footnotes) and interpretation.

1–6. The second Servant Poem. In this, unlike the first and
fourth poems, it is the Servant who speaks, in the form of a
prophet's confession. There are points of resemblance to
Jeremiah which can hardly be accidental. He is designated
from birth for his task, with a message both for Israel and for
the nations; he knows failure and reassurance from God, and
it is precisely in his recognition of utter dependence on God
that he learns the greatness of his role in the divine purpose.

1. *called...named*: cp. 43: 1; *from my mother's womb*: cp.
44: 2; 46: 3.

2. *tongue*: literally 'mouth'. The mouth was the distinctive organ of the prophet's function (cp. Isa. 6: 7; Jer. 1: 9) as
also of worshipping Israel (cp. Ps. 71: 8). *concealed...hid me
out of sight* may mean that the Servant has for a long time been
unrecognized, but was being prepared by God for his mission.
Or it may mean, using the metaphor that the *sharp sword* is
in the scabbard, the *polished arrow* in the *quiver* (*out of sight* is
not in the Hebrew), ready for action.

3. *my servant, Israel*: this phrase seems to answer the ques-

88

tion 'Who is the Servant?' quite explicitly. But verse 5 gives the Servant a mission to Israel. How can Israel restore Israel? Some who are acutely aware of this apparent contradiction would regard *Israel* in verse 3 as a later addition, but this is not supported by manuscript (including Dead Sea Scroll) evidence or by the ancient versions. Perhaps the difficulty is more apparent than real. It is the function of Israel in the purpose of God to be the agent of the world's salvation. But Israel as it becomes self-conscious in the soul of the prophet has still a function to bring Jacob back to God. (For a fuller discussion see pp. 9-14.) In the words of C. R. North 'the first mission of the Church is to the Church'. *I shall win glory:* cp. 44: 23 ('made Israel his masterpiece') where the same verb is used in Hebrew. In this brilliant paradox, it is the Servant who brings glory to the master.

4. *Once I said* suggests that the Servant said this in the past in contrast to what he is saying now. The Hebrew rather emphasizes 'I' in contrast to 'He' in verse 3. Thus we would translate 'But [in spite of what is said in verse 3] I said...' Then the real truth of the Servant's experience becomes clear as he presents his failure to God. Jeremiah also feared that he had laboured in vain, but he learned that the LORD was on his side (Jer. 20: 7-11). *my cause:* i.e. my true judgement; cp. 1 Cor. 4: 5.

5-6. This is a new word of God to his Servant. The restoration of Israel to its true role involves the bringing of *light* and *salvation* to all mankind; cp. 42: 6.

7. This verse seems to be a reflection on verse 4 and to point forward to Isa. 52: 13 – 53: 12.

8-12. This is an oracle addressed to Israel. The prophet sees himself already in Jerusalem, and the exiles from various parts of the world, including Egypt, returning to the holy city. This is the answer to the prayer 'How long...?' (Pss. 74: 10; 79: 5).

8. This verse is quoted in 2 Cor. 6: 2. The words following *deliverance* appear in the footnote where the difficult phrase

'covenant of the people' is rendered 'a light to all peoples'
as in 42: 6. *sharing out afresh its desolate fields* is a deliberate
allusion to the allotting of the land (the LORD's inheritance)
in the days of the settlement, while the following verses pick
up the theme of exodus wandering.

12. *Syene* is the modern Aswan where a Jewish colony is
referred to in the Elephantine papyri of the fifth century B.C.
(see *Understanding the Old Testament* in this series, p. 88).

13 is another of the hymns of praise in which the works
of nature rejoice in the LORD's saving work. ✷

THE WONDERFUL RESTORATION OF ZION

14   But Zion says,
    'The LORD has forsaken me; my God[a] has forgotten
        me.'
15   Can a woman forget the infant at her breast,
        or a loving mother the child of her womb?
    Even these forget, yet I will not forget you.
16   Your walls are always before my eyes,
        I have engraved them on the palms of my hands.
17   Those who are to rebuild you make better speed
            than those who pulled you down,
        while those who laid you waste depart.
18   Raise your eyes and look around you:
    see how they assemble, how they are flocking back to
        you.
        By my life I, the LORD, swear it,
        you shall wear them proudly as your jewels,
            and adorn yourself with them like a bride;
19   I did indeed make you waste and desolate,
        I razed you to the ground,

[a] my God: *so Scroll; Heb.* the Lord.

but your boundaries*a* shall now be too narrow
  for your inhabitants –
  and those who laid you in ruins are far away.
The children born in your bereavement shall yet say 20
    in your hearing,
'This place is too narrow; make room for me to live
      in.'

    Then you will say to yourself,   21
  'All these children, how did I come by them,
  bereaved and barren as I was?*b*
  Who reared them
  when I was left alone, left by myself;
  where did I get them all?'

  The Lord GOD says,   22
Now is the time: I will beckon to the nations
  and hoist a signal to the peoples,
  and they shall bring your sons in their arms
  and carry your daughters on their shoulders;
  kings shall be your foster-fathers   23
    and their princesses shall be your nurses.
They shall bow to the earth before you
    and lick the dust from your feet;
  and you shall know that I am the LORD
  and that none who look to me will be
      disappointed.
  Can his prey be taken from the strong man,   24
  or the captive be rescued from the ruthless*c*?
    And the LORD answers,   25

[a] I did...boundaries: *or* your wasted and desolate land, your ruined
countryside.   [b] *So Sept.; Heb. adds* an exile and removed.
[c] *So Scroll; Heb.* righteous.

91

> The captive shall be taken even from the strong,
>   and the prey of the ruthless shall be rescued;
> I will contend with all who contend against you
>   and save your children from them.
> 26 I will force your oppressors to feed on their own flesh
>   and make them drunk with their own blood as if with
>   fresh wine,
>   and all mankind shall know
> that it is I, the LORD, who save you,
>   I your ransomer, the Mighty One of Jacob.

✳ The contrast between the prophetic faith and the actual situation can be realized if we recall the description of the fall of Jerusalem in 2 Kings 25: 8–21 and its effect on the Jews expressed in Lamentations. Jerusalem was a devastated city, its temple destroyed, its houses in ruins, and its walls broken down. The poem shows that the prophet is well aware of this. He knows that what he expects is nothing short of miraculous, but he also knows that the LORD who brought about this devastation is about to effect a restoration.

14–16. The despondency of the Jews in Judaea was understandable. The prophet would know how impossible his words in verses 8–13 would sound to those who came to the ruined shrine, chanting the words of Lam. 1. The divine answer is given in two forms. First, God's love goes beyond, and is tenderer than, even a mother's love for her child (verse 15). The metaphor then changes to that of the divine architect whose plans for the new Jerusalem are not written on a perishable tile (Ezek. 4: 1) but are *engraved* (or tattooed) on the palms of his hands.

17. With magnificent hyperbole he declares that Jerusalem will be rebuilt more quickly than it was destroyed. In actual fact even Nehemiah's walls took fifty-two days to complete.

18 picks up the words of verse 12.

19-21. The ruined and abandoned city will suddenly find itself over-populated, an event as unlikely as a widowed or barren woman having a large family.

22-3. The scene now changes to the nations among whom exiled Jews have been living. These humiliated exiles will not simply be allowed to return but will be honourably escorted back. *lick the dust* is a conventional expression meaning 'do homage'.

24 may be Zion's incredulous question to which the divine answer is given in verses 25-6.

26. Israel's *Mighty One* (cp. Gen. 49: 24; Isa. 1: 24) is stronger by far than the ruthless Babylonians. *feed on their own flesh...drunk with their own blood* are again conventional expressions to describe siege conditions. Babylon will be besieged as she besieged Jerusalem. The divine purpose in this act of deliverance is first that Israel shall know, and then that all mankind shall know, that the LORD is God (this verse and verse 23). ✻

ISRAEL'S SEPARATION FROM GOD

The LORD says,   **50**
Is there anywhere a deed of divorce
    by which I have put your mother away?
    Was there some creditor of mine
    to whom I sold you?
No; it was through your own wickedness that you
        were sold
and for your own misconduct that your mother was
        put away.
Why, then, did I find no one when I came?   2
    Why, when I called, did no one answer?
Did you think my arm too short to redeem,
    did you think I had no power to save?

93

Not so. By my rebuke I dried up the sea
   and turned rivers into desert;
   their fish perished for lack of water
     and died on the thirsty ground;
3   I clothed the skies in mourning
   and covered them with sackcloth.

✻ There seems to be no sequence of thought between the three sections of ch. 50. Verses 1–3 might be connected with 49: 14–21 and again with ch. 54. In these verses Israel's relationship with God is likened to that of a marriage. On Israel's side this has been destroyed; the exile was the consequence. But the separation was not, like a divorce, final. God is determined to restore Israel (cp. Hos. 1–3) and has made this plain by the word of the prophet. Why then is there no response? Does Israel suppose that God has 'no power to save'? Let them consider the power of God in the cataclysms of the world of nature.

1. The words are apparently addressed to the exiles (*your . . . you*) who found the oracles beyond belief. *mother* refers to Jerusalem. The charge is against those who complained that God had forgotten them or that he was impotent (40: 27; 49: 14). There had been no divorce, for there was no written document such as the Law required (Deut. 24: 1); God was not indebted to anyone, so the children of Israel were not sold to meet the father's debts (cp. 2 Kings 4: 1).

2. *redeem* translates a word which, unlike that for ransom, emphasizes payment or buying back. *perished:* literally 'are dried up', a slight emendation of the Hebrew text which has 'stink'; this may be a reference to the plague judgements on Egypt (Exod. 7: 21) and would be appropriate to a similar allusion in verse 3 which describes the heavy black clouds, a symbol of the coming of God for judgement. ✻

A CONFESSION OF TRUST IN GOD

The Lord GOD has given me 4
the tongue of a teacher
and skill to console the weary
with a word*a* in the morning;
he sharpened my hearing*b*
that I might listen like one who is taught.
The Lord GOD opened my ears 5
and I did not disobey or turn back in defiance.
I offered my back to the lash, 6
and let my beard be plucked from my chin,
I did not hide my face from spitting and insult;
but the Lord GOD stands by to help me; 7
therefore no insult can wound me.
I have set my face like flint,
for I know that I shall not be put to shame,
because one who will clear my name is at my side. 8
Who dare argue against me? Let us confront one
another.
Who will dispute my cause? Let him come forward.
The Lord GOD will help me; 9
who then can prove me guilty?
They will all wear out like a garment,
the moths will eat them up.

✻ This is the third Servant Poem. In spite of violent opposition the Servant knows that God helps him and will vindicate
him (cp. Luke 18: 7). He will resolutely fulfil his God-given

[a] *Prob. rdg.*, *cp. Sept.*; *Heb. adds* he bores in the morning.
[b] sharpened my hearing: *lit.* bored my ears.

task, cost what it may, convinced that he will succeed at God's command and by God's help. The shame he has endured is not a sign of divine condemnation, as men judge. Rather is God on his side; it is the opponents who will be defeated. How this reversal will come, and what form it will take, is not explained. The strange victory is declared in the fourth poem, 52: 13 – 53: 12. In this poem there are many points of resemblance to Jeremiah's confessions (cp. Jer. 20: 7–13), and to Job's protestation of innocence (cp. Job 30f.) and the psalms in which the individual cries out to God for help, e.g. Ps. 22.

4. *teacher:* the Hebrew word is plural, and at the end of the verse is translated *one who is taught*; in Jer. 13: 23 it is translated 'you who are schooled'; cp. Isa. 8: 16; Isa. 54: 13: 'instructed'. The N.E.B. apparently understands *teacher* as 'an effective teacher' and parallel to 'one who is skilled' (see next clause). It may be better to translate the one Hebrew word which occurs twice in the verse by a similar English equivalent, perhaps 'those who are well taught' which would suit the following clause and be consistent with the last word in the sentence, 'like those who are well taught'.

6. *my back:* cp. Ps. 129: 3. *my beard be plucked:* a gross insult, cp. 2 Sam. 10: 4.

8. The Servant challenges his opponents to meet him before the judge. ✳

THE FAITHFUL AND THE FAITHLESS

10   Which of you fears the LORD and obeys his servant's
            commands?
        The man who walks in dark places with no light,
        yet trusts in the name of the LORD and leans on his God.
11   But you who kindle a fire and set fire-brands alight,[a]
        go, walk into your own fire
        and among the fire-brands you have set ablaze.

[a] set...alight: *prob. rdg., cp. Sept.; Heb.* gird on fire-brands.

96

> This is your fate at my hands:
>   you shall lie down in torment.

✳ This brief poem is somewhat obscure, expecially in verse
11. Verse 10 seems to be an appeal to those who have almost
lost hope during the long days of Babylonian domination,
while still clinging to something of their ancient faith. They
may yet pay heed to the Servant. Then verse 11 may refer to
apostate Jews who are stirring up strife. They will perish in the
fire they have made. Verse 10 could be translated 'Who
among you fears and obeys...walks in dark places...let him
trust'. ✳

SALVATION IS AT HAND

✳ Isa. 51: 1 – 52: 2 may be read as one poem in two parts
with the general theme of deliverance, or more probably as
two poems: 51: 1–16 whose three stanzas are introduced by
'Listen' or 'Pay heed to me', and 51: 17 – 52: 2 whose three
stanzas begin with 'Awake, Awake.' Others would see here
six or more independent poems of varying length, assembled
by the catchwords 'Listen', 'Pay heed', 'Awake'. ✳

> Listen to me, all who follow the right and seek the **51**
>   LORD:
>   look to the rock from which you were hewn,
>   to the quarry from which you were dug;
>   look to your father Abraham   2
>   and to Sarah who gave you birth:
> when I called him he was but one,
>   I blessed him and made him many.
>   The LORD has indeed comforted Zion,   3
>   comforted all her ruined homes,
>   turning her wilderness into an Eden,
>   her thirsty plains into a garden of the LORD.

97

Joy and gladness shall be found in her,
   thanksgiving and melody.
4   Pay heed to me, my people,[a]
   and hear me, O my nation;[b]
   for my law shall shine forth
and I will flash the light of my judgement over the
         nations.
5 My victory is near, my deliverance has gone[c] forth
      and my arm shall rule the nations;
   for me coasts and islands shall wait
      and they shall look to me for protection.

6   Lift your eyes to the heavens,
   look at the earth beneath:
   the heavens grow murky as smoke;
   the earth wears into tatters like a garment,
   and those who live on it die like maggots;
   but my deliverance is everlasting
      and my saving power shall never wane.

7   Listen to me, my people who know what is right,
   you who lay my law to heart:
      do not fear the taunts of men,
      let no reproaches dismay you;
8   for the grub will devour them like a garment
   and the moth as if they were wool,
   but my saving power shall last for ever
      and my deliverance to all generations.

9   Awake, awake, put on your strength, O arm of the Lord,
   awake as you did long ago, in days gone by.

[a] my people: *or, with some MSS.,* peoples.
[b] O my nation: *or, with some MSS.,* O nations.
[c] *Or* shone.

98

Was it not you
who hacked the Rahab in pieces and ran the dragon
through?
Was it not you   10
who dried up the sea, the waters of the great abyss,
and made the ocean depths a path for the ransomed?
So the LORD's people shall come back, set free,   11
and enter Zion with shouts of triumph,
crowned with everlasting joy;
joy and gladness shall overtake them as they come,
and sorrow and sighing shall flee away.
I, I myself, am he that comforts you.   12
Why then fear man, man who must die,
man frail as grass?
Why have you forgotten the LORD your maker,   13
who stretched out the skies and founded the earth?
Why are you continually afraid, all the day long,
why dread the fury of oppressors ready to destroy you?
Where is that fury?
He that cowers under it shall soon stand upright and   14
not die,
he shall soon reap the early crop and not lack bread.

I am the LORD your God, the LORD of Hosts is my   15
name. I cleft the sea and its waves roared, that I might   16
fix the heavens in place and form the earth and say to
Zion, 'You are my people.' I have put my words in
your mouth and kept you safe under the shelter of my hand.

✵ 1–3. Remember God's work, beginning with Abraham.
This will enable you to prepare for the fulfilment of his
purpose in the restoration and transformation of Zion.

1. *follow the right*: the Hebrew words recall the command in Deut. 16: 20: 'Justice, and justice alone, you shall pursue.' This would suggest that the appeal is to those who are genuinely seeking the divine requirements as they are declared in Deuteronomy. There is reason to believe that that book, or its teaching, was a dominant factor in the life of loyal Jews who remained in Judaea during and after the exile period. The appeal then may be addressed to Zion (verse 3) where righteousness once dwelt (Isa. 1: 21, 26). They have sought the LORD but apparently their prayers have not been answered. They are then recalled to the faith of Abraham, whose faith was counted as righteousness (Gen. 15: 6) and he received the great promise and blessing (verse 2). Others translate the phrase 'pursue deliverance' (the Revised Standard Version), i.e. God's saving righteousness, and the word is translated 'deliverance' in verses 5, 6 and 8. But the phrase 'pursue deliverance' seems unnatural.

3 seems to be a deliberate allusion to Jer. 7: 34.

4–5. These verses refer back to 42: 1–4. The N.E.B. footnotes to this verse, indicating plural forms, may well represent the correct readings. The word for nation is not otherwise used of Israel. The plurals 'peoples' and 'nations' occur in some Hebrew manuscripts and a Syriac translation. These verses may be seen as the fulfilment of the hymn in Isa. 2: 2–4.

6. Heaven and earth will pass away, but God's *saving power* will endure for ever.

7–8. These verses are addressed to Zion in its humiliation. They *know* the divine righteousness; God's torah (*law*) is in the *heart* (Deut. 30: 14).

9–14. This is a prayer to God uttered by the prophet in the name of the community in the conventional language of the Psalms; cp. Ps. 44: 23. A brief reference is made to the ancient Canaanite creation myth, as in Ps. 74: 13f. 'Rahab...dragon' are alternative words for the chaos monster; cp. Job 26: 12; Ps. 89: 10. In the Babylonian form of the myth the chaos monster was defeated by Marduk after a great combat. In Second Isaiah, as in the Psalms, the myth is transformed by equating 'the waters of the great abyss' with the waters of the Red Sea through which Israel passed in safety. This in turn became the symbol for the deliverance of the exiles. Again, here the prophet uses exodus themes to draw out the nature of God's new action for his people. Thus the prayer merges into a hymn of praise (verse 11) and a renewal of confidence in the Creator and Saviour. Verses 12–14 contain the divine answer to the prayer.

14. The exact translation of this verse varies in the early versions and in English (cp. the Authorized Version and the Revised Standard Version). The general meaning is that the oppressed will be set free and have sufficient food. The conclusion seems rather lame until one recalls the utter dependence of the inhabitants of Palestine on the harvest.

15–16 appear to be a prose summary of 9–14 and in the last sentence use words that are reminiscent of the Servant Poems, 49: 2; 50: 4. The N.E.B. has rearranged the clauses (cp. the Revised Standard Version). If the order of the clauses in the Hebrew text is retained we may read these verses as the divine answer to those who have 'forgotten the LORD' and 'are continually afraid' (verse 13), and a poetic structure can be discerned.

> 'I am the LORD your God
>> cleaving the sea and its waves roared
>> (the Lord of Hosts is his name)
> I have put my words in your mouth
>> and in the shadow of my hand I have covered you
> Fixing the heavens in place,
>> laying the foundation of the earth,
>> and saying to Zion: "You are my people."'

The essential thought is 'He who has chosen you is the Creator and the Preserver of his people.' *

THE CUP OF JUDGEMENT

17   Awake, awake; rise up, Jerusalem.
     You have drunk from the LORD's hand
       the cup of his wrath,
       drained to its dregs the bowl of drunkenness;
18   of all the sons you have borne there is not one to guide
          you,
     of all you have reared, not one to take you by the
          hand.
19   These two disasters have overtaken you;
       who can console you?–
    havoc and ruin, famine and the sword;
       who can comfort you[a]? –
20   Your sons are in stupor, they lie at the head of every
          street,
       like antelopes caught in the net,
       glutted with the wrath of the LORD,
       the rebuke of your God.
21   Therefore listen to this, in your affliction,
       drunk that you are, but not with wine:
22   thus says the LORD, your Lord and your God,
       who will plead his people's cause:
     Look, I take from your hand
       the cup of drunkenness;
    you shall never again drink from the bowl of my
       wrath,
23   I will give it instead to your tormentors and
       oppressors,[b]

[a] who can comfort you: *so Scroll; Heb.* who am I to comfort you.
[b] and oppressors: *so Scroll; Heb. om.*

those who said to you, 'Lie down and we will walk
over you';
and you made your backs like the ground beneath
them,
like a roadway for passers-by.

Awake, awake, put on your strength, O Zion,   **52**
put on your loveliest garments, holy city of Jerusalem;
for never shall the uncircumcised and the unclean enter
you again.
Rise up, captive Jerusalem, shake off the dust;   2
loose your neck from the collar that binds it,
O captive daughter of Zion.

* This is a call to Jerusalem, i.e. the people of God about to
be restored. They are in despair, and will remain so until they
recognize the harsh truth that their condition is not due to
chance nor ultimately to the violence of the invader, but to
the judgement of God. Terrifying though that thought is, it is
also the one ground for hope, since divine judgement leads
to salvation. Among those who remained in Judaea the same
thought was being expressed in Lam. 3. These verses in Isaiah
may be seen as the prophetic answer to the ritual lament.
Grieve indeed, but prepare now for the fulfilment of God's
purpose, his work of vindication.

18. The metaphor suddenly changes to that of a childless
widow.

19. *two disasters:* a devastated land, and a people suffering
from invasion.

21–3 is the reversal of the past misfortunes of Jerusalem.
The pronouns are second person feminine singular, i.e. the
city. The prophet's oracle begins in verse 22, in a particularly
solemn form: *thus says your Lord, Yahweh, your God, who
will plead his people's cause.* The suffering Jerusalem has

endured will now be at an end for her and will pass to the oppressing Babylon.

52: 1–2. Although it is the same call, *Awake*, the note now is one of exultant joy. After the judgement comes the restoration. This is not for some distant future but is now; the Kingdom of God is at hand. Jerusalem is about to be set free from foreign domination and from the ritual impurity which that involved. She is to prepare to meet God, adorned for a joyous festival occasion. *put on your strength:* literally 'clothe yourself with your strength'. The unusual metaphor is the same as that in 51: 9 where it refers to armour. Since *captive Jerusalem* obviously has no strength, we must suppose that she is to put on the strength which God supplies, that which derives from the covenant relationship which the LORD has renewed. ✳

YOUR GOD RULES

3 The LORD says, You were sold but no price was paid,
4 and without payment you shall be ransomed. The Lord
GOD says, At the beginning my people went down into
Egypt to live there, and at the end it was the Assyrians
5 who oppressed them; but now what do I find here? says
the LORD. My people carried off and no price paid, their
rulers derided, and my name reviled all day long, says
6 the LORD. But on that day my people shall know my
name;[a] they shall know that it is I who speak; here I am.

7   How lovely on the mountains are the feet of the herald
who comes to proclaim prosperity and bring good
news,
the news of deliverance,
calling to Zion, 'Your God is king.'

[a] *So Sept.; Heb. adds* therefore.

Hark, your watchmen raise their voices   8
    and shout together in triumph;
for with their own eyes they shall see
the LORD returning in pity[a] to Zion.
Break forth together in shouts of triumph,   9
    you ruins of Jerusalem;
for the LORD has taken pity on his people
    and has ransomed Jerusalem.
The LORD has bared his holy arm   10
    in the sight of all nations,
and the whole world from end to end
shall see the deliverance of our God.
Away from Babylon; come out, come out,   11
    touch nothing unclean.
Come out from Babylon, keep yourselves pure,
    you who carry the vessels of the LORD.
But you shall not come out in urgent haste   12
    nor leave like fugitives;
for the LORD will march at your head,
    your rearguard will be Israel's God.

✶ Verses 3–6, or at least 4–6, are in prose.
  3 appears to be a brief oracle of which the remaining verses are an explanation of the *no price* and *without payment* (the N.E.B. omits 'for nothing' at the end of verse 4 where the Septuagint has a similar-sounding word meaning 'with violence'. Apparently the Septuagint is accepted and the final word included in 'oppressed them'). The whole period of Israel's history before the Babylonian invasion is presented as beginning and ending with foreign domination. But now 'my people' have been taken away from the land which God

[a] in pity: *so Scroll; Heb. om.*

105

appointed for them, as though to prove that Israel's God was impotent. The day of release is dawning. Israel will know that he who speaks by the prophet is that sovereign LORD.

7–12 is a hymn which celebrates the LORD's triumphant return to Zion leading his people from captivity into a new freedom. Jerusalem is to be liberated; the exiles will bring back the sacred vessels in readiness for the restoration of the temple worship. All mankind will recognize the Day of the LORD's victory. The hymn picks up the familiar themes of the psalms which celebrate the sovereignty of God: Pss. 47; 93; 96–9. Here is another use of the exodus theme, but this will be an exodus more wonderful than that from Egypt (verse 12). ✻

HUMILIATION AND VICTORY OF THE SERVANT

13   Behold, my servant shall prosper,[a]
    he shall be lifted up, exalted to the heights.

14   Time was when many[b] were aghast at you, my people;[c]
15   so now many nations[d] recoil at sight of him,
    and kings curl their lips in disgust.
    For they see what they had never been told
        and things unheard before fill their thoughts.

53   Who could have believed what we have heard,
    and to whom has the power of the LORD been revealed?

2   He grew up before the LORD like a young plant
    whose roots are in parched ground;
    he had no beauty, no majesty to draw our eyes,
        no grace to make us delight in him;
    his form, disfigured, lost all the likeness of a man,
        his beauty changed beyond human semblance.[e]

[a] prosper: *or, with slight change,* be bound.　[b] *Or the great.*　[c] *See note on 53: 2.*　[d] *Or great nations.*　[e] his form...semblance: *transposed from end of 52: 14.*

He was despised, he shrank from the sight of men, 3
　　tormented and humbled by suffering;
　　　we despised him,*a* we held him of no account,
　　　a thing from which men turn away their eyes.
Yet on himself he bore our sufferings, 4
　　our torments he endured,
　　while we counted him smitten by God,
　　　struck down by disease and misery;
　　but he was pierced for our transgressions, 5
　　　tortured for our iniquities;
　　the chastisement he bore is health for us
　　　and by his scourging we are healed.
We had all strayed like sheep, 6
each of us had gone his own way;
　　but the Lord laid upon him
　　　the guilt of us all.
He was afflicted, he submitted to be struck down 7
　　and did not open his mouth;
　　he was led like a sheep to the slaughter,
　　like a ewe that is dumb before the shearers.*b*
Without protection, without justice,*c* he was taken 8
　　　　　away;
　　and who gave a thought to his fate,
　　　how he was cut off from the world of living men,
　　stricken to the death*d* for my people's transgression?
He was assigned a grave with the wicked, 9
a burial-place*e* among the refuse of mankind,

[a] we despised him: *so Scroll; Heb.* one despised.
[b] *Prob. rdg.; Heb. adds* and he would not open his mouth.
[c] Without protection, without justice: *or* After arrest and sentence.
[d] stricken to the death: *so Sept.; Heb.* a plague for him.
[e] a burial-place: *so Scroll; Heb.* in his deaths.

    though he had done no violence
      and spoken no word of treachery.

10   Yet the LORD took thought for his tortured servant
    and healed him who had made himself[a] a sacrifice for
      sin;[b]
    so shall he enjoy long life and see his children's children,
      and in his hand the LORD's cause shall prosper.

11   After all his pains he shall be bathed in light,[c]
    after his disgrace he shall be fully vindicated;
    so shall he, my servant, vindicate many,
      himself bearing the penalty of their guilt.

12   Therefore I will allot him a portion with the great,
      and he shall share the spoil with the mighty,
    because he exposed himself to face death[d]
      and was reckoned among transgressors,
    because he bore the sin of many
      and interceded for their transgressions.

✻ This, usually denoted the fourth Servant Poem, is surely
the best known and most frequently quoted passage in Second
Isaiah and deservedly so for the sublimity of its poetry and its
theological profundity. Jewish scholars have, with justification, seen it as portraying the sufferings of the Jews down
through the centuries. Christians, from New Testament days
onwards, have seen this poem above all others as fulfilled in
the life, death and resurrection of Jesus, and therefore also of
the community of his followers, the Church, in the purpose
of God. By this is meant not that the passage is a blue-print
whose every detail was to be slavishly followed, but as an

[a] healed…himself: *prob. rdg.; Heb.* he made sick, if you make.
[b] sacrifice for sin: *lit.* guilt-offering.
[c] light: *so Scroll; Heb. om.*
[d] *Or* because he poured out his life to the death.

expression of the mind and purpose of God for his Servant. It is a work of art such as only a great prophet and poet could write.

This is both the tragic experience and the supreme triumph of the loyal, faithful and obedient Servant in a world which ignores God, but a world which God is resolved to save and reconcile to himself. Little wonder then that it has continuously enriched the piety of the faithful and engaged the attention of the scholar.

In broad outline the teaching of the poem is clear. The Servant, humiliated and suffering, is seen as one who is afflicted by God. This can only be as a consequence of sin. Suddenly this is seen as due to 'our transgressions', i.e. what 'we' ought to have suffered. This fate has been voluntarily accepted by the Servant as the means whereby God will reconcile 'us'. It is a vicarious suffering and death for the salvation of the world. This incredible fact is what God himself has chosen for his Servant in order that the many may be brought to him. The Servant is no longer the messenger; he is the agent of the divine work of reconciliation. The only way by which this can be accomplished is by a willing acceptance of suffering and death for others.

Two further comments may be made. (1) This is not substitution as that word is commonly understood, any more than 'a sacrifice for sin' is a substitute for the offerer. The Servant identified himself with godless mankind in its pitiful need, in order that godless mankind might identify itself with his loyal obedience to God. Through him mankind is reconciled to God. (2) This is prophecy in the full meaning of the word. It is the declaration of God's purpose which can be realized only in a life. In detail there are difficulties both in translation and interpretation. These difficulties were felt in the most ancient translations, in early Jewish and Christian versions (as in the Targum, Septuagint and Vulgate) as well as in the various English translations. The N.E.B. footnotes indicate some of the problems for a translator, as will a

comparison with the Revised Standard Version. The Hebrew
has a remarkable number of words and phrases which are not
otherwise found in Isa. 40–55, some of which are rare in Old
Testament usage. This alone may indicate the mental struggle
of the prophet/poet to put into the language of man that
which he had received. The prophet has received more than
he can understand; the poet must try to say more than
language, even that of the lament psalms, can express. It also
indicates the difficulties of rendering the Hebrew poem into
equivalent English. Only a prophet could 'see' and 'hear';
only a poet could 'say'. Only the mind that has been opened
by the divine work of reconciliation can receive.

The poem falls into three sections. (A) 52: 13–15. God
proclaims the exaltation and vindication of his Servant. (B)
53: 1–9. Confession of the nations; they could not recognize
in this humiliated, unprepossessing figure, who was not only
rejected by men but smitten by God and lacking any divine
favour, one in whom God was at work to effect their atonement. Now at last they see that it was for their sins that he
suffered, that he had voluntarily accepted the suffering for the
sins of the world, and that this was for the healing of the
nations. The language of this section recalls that of Pss. 22; 88.
(C) The divine declaration, 53: 10–12. The loyal obedience
of the Servant becomes the medium through which the divine
purpose will be accomplished. This is the Servant's victory, as
it is the triumph of the divine purpose. The apparent rejection
of the Servant by God, voluntarily accepted, is the means by
which a rebellious world will be restored to fellowship with
God. Thus the poem containing the confession (B) is set
within the framework of the divine vindication (A and
C).

52: 13–15. The divine proclamation: the rejected Servant
will be exalted. This introductory section presents a total
reversal from humiliation to exaltation of the Servant. His
mission, apparently a failure, will be a complete success.
What the nations and their kings could not see will be revealed

in a moment of illumination. At last the ultimate significance
of the earlier servant poems becomes clear. Obviously this is,
at the moment, apparent only to the prophet, but it is the
reality behind the appearances into which first his hearers and
eventually all will be drawn.

13. *Behold, my servant:* cp. 42: 1. *prosper:* the primary
meaning of the Hebrew is 'deal wisely' (Authorized Version,
Revised Version) but it is an effective wisdom as in Josh. 1: 8,
'be successful'. The footnote rendering supposes an alternative
translation that is philologically possible but less suitable to
the context. *exalted to the heights:* a daring phrase, reminiscent
of phrases associated with God (Ps. 57: 5, 11) and intended to
mean above all human dignity. The language is reflected in
Phil. 2: 9.

14. See N.E.B. footnotes *c* and *d*. If the words rendered in
the footnotes are retained here they should be read in parenthesis as a preparation for what follows in ch. 53. *my people*
is not in the Hebrew of this verse. It appears to be an attempt
to account for *at you* where one would expect 'at him'. The
effect is to distinguish between 'my servant' or 'him' and
Israel. But this transition from a second person to third person
occurs elsewhere, e.g. 45: 21 (see N.E.B. footnote), although
it could hardly be reproduced in English usage. It might be
better to keep to the third person singular throughout.

15. *recoil* corresponds to a verb which normally means 'to
sprinkle something on' (cp. the Authorized Version and the
Revised Version); here however the English would be understood as sprinkling (water or blood) on many nations. But
this is not a legitimate rendering of words which could only
mean 'sprinkle many nations on something'! The following
line supports the N.E.B. suggestion which may be based on a
similar Arabic word or a slight emendation. Otherwise we
must accept the unusual meaning 'besprinkle' and suppose
that *many nations* perform a purificatory rite upon the Servant.
This would destroy the sequence of thought in the verse
and the parallelism of the first two lines. The last two lines

indicate the unexpectedness of God's reversal of fortune for his Servant.

53: 1–9. The nation's confession. What they now see confounds all expectations. Verses 2 and 3 describe what was apparent to all, while verse 1 prepares the way for a true understanding.

1–2. *to whom:* literally 'upon whom'. Can it really be true that one so humiliated and despised is the one upon whom God's victorious power rests? Here the word *revealed* is important and refers back to the divine proclamation in 52: 13–15. In some mysterious way, God has made known to them the truth about the Servant. Nothing short of revelation could account for this new understanding; cp. Matt. 16: 17. The description that follows is not to be taken literally. It tells of one who, by every reasonable judgement in the ancient world, is the object of divine displeasure and therefore to be avoided by others; cp. Job 30: 5, 10. The suggestion that the Servant was a leper is inappropriate.

3. *humbled:* the Hebrew verb was earlier translated 'acquainted' but is now recognized by many scholars as meaning 'humiliated' as also in verse 11, 'his disgrace'.

4–6. This new estimate of the Servant's sufferings could only come from the converted. The contrasts between the new and the old judgements are vividly presented, and lead to the confession of sin in verse 6. The sufferer is not the sinner; the sinner is not the sufferer. The Servant suffered for the sins of others, and by his sufferings brought about a total restoration of health and well-being ('we are healed') to them. How this could be is not explained (but see verses 10–12). It is accepted as a revolutionary fact in which God himself is involved.

6. *guilt* or 'iniquity'. Sin and its consequences are so closely related that in Hebrew the same word is used.

7–9. The picture here changes from sickness to suffering inflicted by others. The contrasts here are between what he suffered and how he submitted to it. Verse 7 describes his submissive attitude. Verses 8–9 may, but not necessarily, speak of his death. The obvious meaning of the language in these verses is that the Servant has unjustly been put to death and buried in a felon's grave. But a comparison with Ps. 88 may suggest that the language is that of poetry, and intended to convey the extremity of suffering and abandonment by men. Again, Ezekiel describes the condition of the exiled Jews as long dead (Ezek. 37: 1–14, especially verse 11). This means that what seems the obvious interpretation to us, who are not Jews in exile, and do not wholly share their modes of thinking, may not be according to their understanding of the language or the intention of the prophet. Death for them had a wider meaning than physical death. It included serious weakness, both physical and spiritual, approximating to what we might call hopelessness and collapse of morale. Similarly restoration to life, cp. verses 10–12, could mean as in Hos. 6: 2 re-invigoration. Separation from God was death; restoration to fellowship with God was life. This is still the language of Paul in Eph. 2: 1, 5f. This may help us to avoid the suggestions either that the prophet is writing his own obituary or that this poem was written by another (and greater) prophet. In any case the view taken in this commentary is that the Servant is Israel doomed to death, but resurrected by God for the fulfilment of his work of deliverance (cp. pp. 12–14).

8. The precise translation of this verse is uncertain. The N.E.B. text and footnotes should be noted together with the Revised Standard Version. The meaning is, however, clear enough. The Servant has suffered a grave injustice by violence, and no one was concerned about him. *for my people's transgression:* since this is part of a nation's or king's confession, it must be each nation (personified) or king speaking about his own people. Perhaps 'people(s)' without the pronoun should be understood, or, by a small emendation, 'for our transgressions'.

9. *among the refuse of mankind:* this is an emendation of the Hebrew 'with a rich man' (Revised Standard Version). If

the Hebrew text is accepted it means apparently that the Servant will be buried in *wicked* and wealthy Babylon. The parallelism of Hebrew poetry favours the N.E.B. Neither by action nor by speech had the Servant deserved such a fate.

10–12. God's vindication of his suffering Servant. Verse 10 may be read as the prophet's own reflection leading to the divine word of verses 11–12. All that the Servant had endured took place in the divine purpose. The willing acceptance by the Servant makes his experience 'a sacrifice for sin' on behalf of the nations, so that they, being restored to fellowship with God, become part of the family of Israel. The servant shares in the victory of the divine warrior over the evil of the world.

10. *took thought...cause* represent the same word in Hebrew. We might render 'purpose' in both places. The LORD's purpose was that he should be tortured (or crushed)... *in his hand the LORD's* purpose *shall prosper. a sacrifice for sin:* this is a technical term in the cultus, meaning a guilt-offering; cp. Lev. 5: 14 – 6: 7. Properly it would be offered by the offender in recognition of the wrong he has committed against God. It was not a penalty, but a divinely appointed means of restoring the broken relationship. In this passage the concept has been transformed, in that the Servant offers himself on behalf of others, as the means whereby they may be reconciled. (The fact that this term attains prominence only in those parts of the Law which are concerned with sacrifice and ritual may simply mean that it was well known in priestly circles in Jerusalem and therefore familiar to the exiles who were mainly drawn from Jerusalem and included a high proportion of priests.) This, being accepted by God, results in the restoration of the Servant (Israel) and a great posterity (? converts from the nations).

11. *he shall be bathed in light:* 'light' is added here from the Scrolls and the Septuagint, while 'be bathed' is based on a possible understanding of the Hebrew verb which would normally be read as 'see'. *after his disgrace:* 'humiliation' (cp. verse 3), but 'by his knowledge (of God)' would suit the

context equally well. *vindicated...vindicate:* the Servant, himself in a right relationship with God, will be able to bring the *many* into the same relationship by his living relationship with them. *penalty of their guilt:* the word *penalty* is an unnecessary addition. What is meant is that the Servant will bear the burden of their iniquity (or guilt).

12. The opening lines call to mind a triumphant procession after a war, but here the war is against all that alienates man from God. They could also be translated: 'I will allot him the many [i.e. 'all' as in verse 11] as his portion, and he shall share the strong ones as his spoil.' *exposed himself:* i.e. bared himself to the threat of death. The N.E.B. footnote 'poured out his life' adopts an alternative sense of the same Hebrew verb, and in this case 'to the death' virtually means 'completely'. *interceded:* either as prophet or king. He prays for those who have afflicted him. Only one who is wholly devoted to God can so pray for those to whom he has unreservedly given himself. ✲

GOD'S UNFAILING LOVE

Sing aloud, O barren woman who never bore a child, **54**
break into cries of joy, you who have never been in
labour;
for the deserted wife has more sons than she who
lives in wedlock,
says the LORD.
Enlarge the limits of your home,   2
spread wide*a* the curtains of your tent;
let out its ropes to the full
and drive the pegs home;
for you shall break out of your confines right and   3
left,

[a] spread wide: *so Sept.; Heb.* let them spread wide.

> your descendants shall dispossess wide regions,[a]
> and re-people cities now desolate.

4 Fear not; you shall not be put to shame,
> you shall suffer no insult, have no cause to blush.
> It is time to forget the shame of your younger days
> and remember no more the reproach of your
> widowhood;

5 for your husband is your maker, whose name is the
> LORD of Hosts;
> your ransomer is the Holy One of Israel
> who is called God of all the earth.

6 The LORD has acknowledged you a wife again,
> once deserted and heart-broken,
> your God has called you a bride still young
> though once rejected.

7 On the impulse of a moment I forsook you,
> but with tender affection I will bring you home again.

8 In sudden anger
> I hid my face from you for a moment;
> but now have I pitied you with a love which never fails,
> says the LORD who ransoms you.

9 These days recall for me the days of Noah:
> as I swore that the waters of Noah's flood
> should never again pour over the earth,
> so now I swear to you
> never again to be angry with you or reproach you.

10 Though the mountains move and the hills shake,
> my love shall be immovable and never fail,
> and my covenant of peace shall not be shaken.
> So says the LORD who takes pity on you.

[a] wide regions: *or* the nations.

✳ The change of mood between Isa. 53 and 54 is abrupt. Yet if our understanding of the Servant is correct, it is appropriate. The Servant's task is seen to be fulfilled. Nothing can be added to that. But the prophet who has received the revelation can, and indeed must, break into a hymn of praise and lead his people into a confession of faith. It is true that he changes his metaphor into that of the forsaken wife restored and possessing a great family. He has used this metaphor earlier (49: 14–21), and a similar transition occurs in Ps. 113: 7–9. We need to remember that in the ancient world, a woman deserted by her husband and children was not merely an object of pity but of scorn. The prophet/poet presents the paradox of his song, *Sing aloud, O barren woman*, a paradox that is resolved in the third line of verse 1, and can only be justified by the solemn 'says the LORD'. Indeed this phrase is repeated in verses 6 (in the Hebrew), 8 and 10, as though to emphasize the God-given certainty. Thus the incredible triumph of Isa. 53: 10–12 issues into the hymn of praise in 54: 1–10, welcoming the dawn of the New Age.

The various themes in the hymn are held together in the over-all theme of the covenant, likened to the marriage relationship, which is maintained by the enduring and compassionate love of God (cp. Hos. 1–3). Within this there are allusions to the nomadic life of the desert (verse 2), and entry into Canaan (verse 3), and rescue from the Babylonian exile (verses 5–8). The mysterious course of Israel's history is at last brought into a unity through the fulfilment of God's unfailing love.

3. *right and left:* while these words are not meant to be taken prosaically, they would be more expressive in Hebrew than in English, as meaning also 'south and north'. *dispossess* or 'take possession of': the verb occurs frequently in the deuteronomic writing in reference to Israel's possession of Canaan.

6. The exact meaning of this verse is somewhat obscure. It depends on the words translated 'heart-broken' of which the

Hebrew is 'forsaken by spirit'. 'Spirit' is that mysterious energy which, in this context, could mean the power to conceive. Thus the wife, once deserted and barren, and perhaps like Sarah too old, is miraculously restored to youth and given the power to have children. At the end of the verse, Hebrew adds 'says your God', which should be kept because of its effective emphasis.

7. *On the impulse of a moment* sounds, in English, capricious. It is doubtful whether more is meant than 'for a brief moment'; cp. verse 8 where the same word is used, but without the preposition and adjective.

8. *pitied* is a strongly emotional word of which the noun appears in verse 7 as 'tender affection'. *love* emphasizes purpose. It is that love which maintains the covenant relationship.

9. This verse recalls the passage in Gen. 8: 21f. But the universal covenant of *the days of Noah* is here applied to the worshipping community in the new Jerusalem, representing all mankind. ✶

THE NEW JERUSALEM

11   O storm-battered city, distressed and disconsolate,
      now I will set your stones in the finest mortar
        and your foundations in lapis lazuli;
12   I will make your battlements of red jasper*a*
      and your gates of garnet;*b*
      all your boundary-stones shall be jewels.
13   Your masons shall all be instructed by the LORD,
      and your sons shall enjoy great prosperity;
14   and in triumph*c* shall you be restored.
      You shall be free from oppression and have no fears,
      free from terror, and it shall not come near you;

[a] *Or* carbuncle.   [b] *Or* firestone.   [c] *Or* in righteousness.

should any attack you, it will not be my doing,   15
the aggressor, whoever he be, shall perish for his
    attempt.
It was I who created the smith   16
    to fan the coals in the furnace
    and forge weapons each for its purpose,
and I who created the destroyer to lay waste;
but now no weapon made to harm you shall prevail,   17
and you shall rebut every charge brought against you.
    Such is the fortune of the servants of the LORD;
        their vindication comes from me.
        This is the very word of the LORD.

✻ By contrast with its present devastated condition, the new
Jerusalem will be like some fabled city of long ago (cp. Ezek.
28: 13f.) in which the people of God will live securely under
his protection. This passage is the original of which Rev.
21: 10–21 is the development. The materials for its
building will be of the most costly and beautiful. Its builders
will be inspired for their work and the new Jerusalem will be
impregnable. The divine blessing, full of the power of fulfilment, will rest permanently on the servants of the LORD (cp.
Ps. 91).
13. *Your masons:* this correction of the Masoretic Text 'your
sons' is based on the Dead Sea Scroll. The difference in spelling
is only of one vowel. This passage is applied in John 6: 45
to the disciples of Jesus. *triumph:* see the N.E.B. footnote *c*.
The meaning is 'in fulfilment of the will of God' and therefore 'secure'. The same word is translated as 'vindication' in
verse 17.
    15. *perish for his attempt:* literally 'fall on account of you';
i.e. Jerusalem, because it is the work of God, will be the
occasion of the aggressor's downfall.
    16. This verse may seem prosaic until we transpose it into

modern terms. God, and he alone, is the creator of those who fashion weapons of destruction, but those weapons will fail to destroy the new Jerusalem.

17. *the fortune:* literally 'the inheritance', a word usually applied to the land of Canaan but here to the divine protection. ✱

INVITATION TO THE GREAT BANQUET

55   Come, all who are thirsty, come, fetch water;
    come, you who have no food, buy corn and eat;
    come and buy, not for money, not for a price.[a]

2   Why spend money and get what is not bread,
    why give the price of your labour and go unsatisfied?
    Only listen to me and you will have good food to eat,
    and you will enjoy the fat of the land.

3   Come to me and listen to my words,
    hear me, and you shall have life:
    I will make a covenant with you, this time for ever,
    to love you faithfully as I loved David.

4   I made him a witness to all races,
    a prince and instructor of peoples;

5   and you in turn shall summon nations you do not know,
    and nations that do not know you shall come running
       to you,
    because the LORD your God,
    the Holy One of Israel, has glorified you.

6   Inquire of the LORD while he is present,
    call upon him when he is close at hand.

7   Let the wicked abandon their ways
    and evil men their thoughts:

[a] *Prob. rdg.; Heb. adds* wine and milk.

let them return to the LORD, who will have pity on
    them,
    return to our God, for he will freely forgive.
    For my thoughts are not your thoughts,   8
        and your ways are not my ways.
        This is the very word of the LORD.
    For as*a* the heavens are higher than the earth,   9
so are my ways higher than your ways
        and my thoughts than your thoughts;
and as the rain and the snow come down from heaven 10
and do not return until they have watered the earth,
        making it blossom and bear fruit,
and give seed for sowing and bread to eat,
so shall the word which comes from my mouth 11
        prevail;
    it shall not return to me fruitless
without accomplishing my purpose
        or succeeding in the task I gave it.
        You shall indeed go out with joy   12
        and be led forth in peace.
Before you mountains and hills shall break into cries of
        joy,
and all the trees of the wild shall clap their hands,
    pine-trees shall shoot up in place of camel-thorn, 13
        myrtles instead of briars;
    all this shall win the LORD a great name,
        imperishable, a sign for all time.

✵ This chapter should be read not merely as the conclusion
to Second Isaiah but as a climax. It is a triumphant epilogue

[a] as: *so Scroll; Heb. om.*

to the prologue of 40: 1–11 and to all the ensuing chapters. Its dramatic and poetic quality has made it one of the best known passages in the book. For that reason, too, an adequate rendering into English is difficult, not because the language is difficult but because the words and phrases cover an area of meaning which their equivalents in another language do not. It may be useful to compare the N.E.B. with other versions, e.g. the Revised Standard Version and the Jerusalem Bible. There are, as there must be, differences. These differences will help us to appreciate the richness of the language.

Verses 1–7 begin with a series of imperatives and verses 8–13 continue into a series of strong affirmations. The situation is one of urgency and the hearers are to be confirmed in faith to meet the supreme event, the manifestation of God's active rule as the New Age dawns. So the affirmations finish with a word which combines the vision of the New Age with a call to leave Babylon; to return in a great procession to the land from which the divine rule will reach out to the whole world.

Throughout this chapter there is an oscillation between the word of God for which the prophet's lips are the mouthpiece of God (verses 1–5, 8–11), and the prophet's own pastoral ministry (verses 6–7, 12–13). The divine word may be seen as the gracious response of God to Israel's praises, especially as they are expressed in such hymns as in Pss. 93; 96–9 which celebrate the sovereignty of God. This sovereignty is about to be realized: 'The LORD is King' indeed. Verses 1–5 might well be seen as an answer to Ps. 89, although the expectations of Ps. 89: 19–37 are to be realized, not by military conquest or political domination, but by a gathering of all mankind into a community of the people of God. This is the kind of victory which only those who have received and accepted the servant poems can know. The redeemed Israel inherits the covenant with David more gloriously than even David could know.

1–2. The invitation to the banquet by God the King begins

in the form of a parable. The familiar cry of the market place is suddenly transformed (*not for money...*) into a humanly impossible situation. No water- or food-seller talks like that! It should be noted that the water-seller was a familiar figure in the towns of the Near East. Moreover the food is not the subsistence of the poor, but like manna from heaven or the bountiful food of a fertile land which God promised to the desert tribes. The N.E.B. footnote to verse 1 suggests that the passage was understood in terms of Wisdom's invitation to a banquet (cp. Prov. 9: 5–6; Ecclus. 24: 19–21). Echoes of this passage appear in the teaching of Jesus (cp. John 6: 32–5) and in Rev. 22: 17. God identifies himself with his people's sorrow in order to lead them into his victory (cp. Isa. 54: 7f.).

Come, the first word in this verse, is an exclamation in Hebrew. Elsewhere in the Old Testament it is associated with grief and mourning. Its use here may suggest that the sight of the depressed and humiliated people prompts this feeling, but in fact the divine purpose is to reverse the present sorrow completely. *food:* the word so translated in these verses is normally translated 'money', i.e. 'silver' (cp. also the French *argent* = silver, money). The N.E.B. has good philological justification but one may doubt whether the same Hebrew word would have such different meanings in the same verse. Money was not at this date coins; that was a later practice of the Persian period.

3–5. *you shall have life* (cp. John 10: 10). The Hebrew might be translated 'you shall have abundant life'. There is no suggestion that the Davidic monarchy will be restored. Rather, all that was associated with David in 2 Sam. 7: 8–16; 23: 5 and the Psalms celebrating the LORD's anointed will be true for the new Israel. Paul has the same thought in his use of 'Christ in you' (cp. Col. 1: 27) and 'in Christ' (cp. 1 Thess. 2: 14). In this, Second Isaiah goes beyond the prophets before him. *this time* (not in the Hebrew) might suggest that the *covenant* with David had come to an end, and if so should be

omitted. Rather has the covenant been fulfilled with a new
extension by being released into the messianic community,
and so giving a particular depth to the Mosaic covenant or
even to the covenant with Noah; cp. Isa. 54: 9. The new
community will be permanently endowed with spirit, live in
a special relationship with God, and be the mediator between
God and all mankind. *a witness:* this role is not explicitly
ascribed to David in the Old Testament, but since the king,
as the LORD's anointed, is seen as the evidence of God's
effective sovereignty, the role of witness may be seen as
implicit. *prince:* or leader as designated by God. This word was
preferred to 'king' in the ancient tradition (1 Sam. 9: 16;
13: 14). *instructor:* this may be a reference to 'the teaching'
(Ps. 132: 12) but the word would be more appropriate to a
priestly function, which was first and foremost to teach the
law of the LORD (Deut. 33: 10; Jer. 18: 18). Others translate
'commander' which would be consistent with Israel's Davidic
function (Ps. 18: 43).

and you in turn...: as David was to Israel, so the redeemed
Israel will be to the nations, in fulfilment of the ancient covenant formula in Exod. 19: 6. The pronouns in verse 5 (*you,
your*) are singular, i.e. Israel is David, or the Davidic monarchy
comes to fulfilment in Israel. But while the 'David' of the
days before the exile was looked to as a conqueror, this new
'David' is he to whom the *nations* will run because the LORD
is with him. This is his true honour.

6–7. The prophet now turns to the exiles, urging them to
prepare themselves for this new role. *Inquire* is a word associated with the worship of the temple, a summons to approach
God for the Kingdom of God is at hand. The emphasis is not
on the appropriate sacrifice but on repentance. *he is present:*
better, 'lets himself be found'.

8–11. Once more we have a word of the LORD in direct
speech. Each of the verses 8–10 (in verse 10, the first *and* in
Hebrew is the same as *for* in verses 8 and 9) begins with a word
of affirmation, as though they would rebut the fears and

doubts of the hearers, by a word of God himself. *my thoughts* is better understood as 'my plans', which are now about to be fulfilled. What the all-powerful LORD decrees will be effected, whether in the created world or in the life of his people. His *word* is full of the power of him whose purposes are beyond man's grasp, seen in the mysterious powers of nature, but most of all in his work of salvation; cp. 40: 8. This is what gives point to the saying of Jesus in Matt. 24: 35.

12–13. The prophet ends on a pastoral note, as though he would say 'All that has been said is for you. Prepare for the new exodus, far transcending the old.' Verse 12 also begins with the Hebrew word of affirmation. It is the prophet's response to the revelation of God, his word of complete assurance to those for whom he has received it. The *name* of God, his self-revelation, once and for all made known in the exodus, will have a deeper and richer meaning than ever before. ✶

THE TEACHING OF ISAIAH 40–55

The work of salvation

✶ It may be convenient to summarize Second Isaiah's teaching around such words as are associated with salvation understood as an act of deliverance, setting someone free. Clearly, if language is to have any content or meaning, deliverance in this situation must be related to the condition of the exiled Jews. Some forty or fifty years before the prophet spoke, they or their parents had been taken captive from Judaea. A high proportion of them were of priestly families, in whose minds the traditions such as are enshrined in the Psalter and the Law were central – but frustrated. If we would do justice to the prophet's hearers we might begin by reading Lamentations (a series of laments recited at the ruined shrine) and Pss. 74; 79; 137, the last of which comes directly from the exiles. Obviously many remembered sadly these ancient traditions and practices. Religious habits die hard, but there was no future. Even if the Babylonian Empire was crumbling before the victorious armies of the Persian king, there was no reason to suppose that the exiled Jews would benefit. The message of the prophet was first that their God would deliver them from the exile and restore them to Jerusalem. This is unambiguously proclaimed in the Prologue (40: 1–11 etc.). Most commonly it is presented in terms of the ancient tradition of the exodus from Egypt, but in language that surpasses all that was associated with the exodus (55: 12f.). It will be effected, not by a group of fugitives, but openly and at the initiative, under God, of the pagan king (44: 28), and supported by the pagan nations (49: 22). The desert will be transformed into a veritable paradise (41: 18f.: cp. ch. 35 for this theme). But deliverance goes deeper than release from exile. It includes that total liberty that can only come in forgiveness of sins and the restoration of that relationship with God wherein Israel's true well-being (peace) consists (44: 22). Israel had indeed sinned, departed from, and rebelled against, God; she had suffered the inevitable consequences, doubly so because she had claimed, and rightly claimed, to have been chosen by God and had broken that relationship. Yet the 'marriage' which only the husband can terminate (Deut. 24: 1–4) remains, because the divine husband has not divorced Israel (50: 1), He will reconcile the unfaithful 'wife' and bring her home with 'tender affection' (54: 7). This work of deliverance will culminate in the restoration of ruined Jerusalem to which the purified people, invigorated by Yahweh's spirit, will return (44: 3), and live again in an intimate relationship with God ('know me') and in faith (43: 10). ✳

The saviour

✳ It is emphasized that this work of deliverance is the work of Yahweh, God of Israel. The epithets and descriptive phrases used of him draw attention to this. He is 'your' or 'our' God, the LORD who is coming in might, the Holy One, creator of the wide world, your ransomer (redeemer),

Jacob's King, your creator, victorious deliverer, first and last. Some of the epithets are traditional. Others are distinctive in these chapters. But by bringing them all together, and proclaiming them to a people who have gradually become convinced that their God has either abandoned them or is impotent before the mighty gods of their conquerors, the prophet manifests his own triumphant faith and remarkable message. If Yahweh is to rescue his people under the very eyes of Babylon's gods, then clearly it is not they but he who is the sovereign lord of men and nations. Other prophets had, it is true, spoken of him as bringing the armies of the great powers to discipline his people. But now, at the very centre of the empire where Babylon's gods were worshipped with great ceremonial, Yahweh acts to deliver his people. The most striking illustrations of this are the reference to Cyrus as the king whom Yahweh has raised up, anointed him (45: 1) as if he were a ruler of the Davidic line, and given him victories in order that he might restore Israel to Jerusalem. Further, this is what Marduk, the great god of Babylon, could not do, nor could Nabu foretell. There is nothing theoretical about these statements. The prophet points to events of history and to the events that Israel is to know at first hand.

The prophet goes further. The whole world is to witness and participate in this work of salvation. In the very city where, with magnificent ritual, the great creation myth was recited celebrating Marduk's victory over chaos, Second Isaiah declares that Yahweh alone brought the world into being, ruling unchallenged and with supreme wisdom the vast vault of heaven with its mysterious stars no less than the earth with its innumerable inhabitants and even the fearful desert. This portrayal of God as Creator is one of the most distinctive contributions of Second Isaiah. It has often been described as 'explicit monotheism'; but the phrase is less than adequate. It could be used for the inference we draw, and rightly draw, from the prophet's words, but his interests are religious rather than philosophical. There have been many monotheisms in the world, normally the reduction of many gods as aspects of one deity, either as supreme among many or as the unknown or unknowable behind all phenomena. Israel's approach, reaching full expression in this prophet, is to acknowledge Yahweh alone as the ruler of history, primarily Israel's but necessarily, since Israel's history is seen as involved in the history of mankind, all history including Creation (the first) and the End (the last). But this leaves nothing for any other god to do! Therefore the gods are impotent, useless nothings, unable to do or foretell anything even for their worshippers. They are as impotent as the material from which their images are made. That is why Second Isaiah ridicules the worship of idols, for idols are genuine symbols – of nothing! But Yahweh has demonstrated his power throughout Israel's history, notably in the exodus in which Israel was created. He is about to act in an even more wonderful way, and the appearance of Cyrus to destroy the power of Babylon is clear evidence of the effectiveness of Yahweh's word. The LORD is the great King, not some remote despot. He is one who ransoms the people whom he has chosen. The word 'ransom' (of God's action) is used more frequently in these chapters than in any book of the Old Testament except for the Psalms. Noun and verb carry with them the thought of the strong member of the family accepting the obligation of coming to the help of a weak member. It suggests the love and loyalty of God for his people in their utter need. At the beginning of Israel's history this is what characterized Yahweh (Exod. 15: 13). In this exile situation, and as Israel is led into the New Age, the Saviour King is best known as 'He who ransoms!' Recent events have brought the word 'ransom' back into popular usage. Provided we think of the one who pays rather than the amount paid, the word is appropriate as a description of him who chose Israel to be his son, his people, and will not 'cast you off' (41: 9). ✻

The saved community

✻ Not only in the 'Servant Poems' but elsewhere in these chapters Israel is described as the Lord's servant, particularly in chs. 41–8. The actual term is not, of course, used elsewhere in the Old Testament exclusively of Israel. It is used of Moses, Joshua, David, Isaiah, the prophets, Nebuchadnezzar, Israel (the whole people). A servant (or slave) is one who carries out his master's will. He may be in a position of trust, or the word may depict him as a loyal worshipper. As used in these chapters the significance of this phrase must be determined by the context. It means Israel, and especially the exiled community, chosen by God, and carried by him 'from the womb' (46: 3); i.e. from its very beginning Israel was the object of Yahweh's care and protection, and will remain so till the end of history. Blind and deaf indeed, yet the servant is still God's messenger, even at the time of humiliation (42: 18–25), and witness to the uniqueness of Yahweh (43: 10 where 'servants' in the Hebrew is in the singular). The rebellious servant has been forgiven, in order that once more God may be seen to be with him (44: 21–3). The world-shaking events which the victories of Cyrus have inaugurated are essentially to rescue Israel in order that all the world may 'know the Lord'.

If to this we add the Servant Poems (see pp. 9–14) this portrait of Israel as the saved community is given further depth. The function of Israel in the purpose of God is, at whatever cost, to make known the way of life in human society that God requires (42: 1–4, 'justice' and 'teaching') and to offer himself, suffering to the point of death, as the one through whom mankind may be reconciled to God – the victory of God and the triumph of the Servant (52: 13 – 53: 12).

The prophet's message refers to the past, sometimes to the remote past of the patriarchal period and the exodus from Egypt. He is remarkably free from sentimental nostalgia in his use of the ancient traditions, but uses them as a jumping-off point for his message. He is fully aware of the immediate past and the follies that led to it, but again this furnishes the context of the situation to which he must address himself. Two matters concern him, as they concern God whose mouthpiece he is – the present condition of his people and that imminent future which at all times conditions his word to the present. The weakness and humiliation, and helplessness, forsakenness and despair of the exiles is what he knows at first hand. Only by entering fully into his people's experience could he deliver to them that which he had received. Like Paul who lived long after his day, he knew what it was to be perplexed yet not to despair (2 Cor. 4: 8f.). Something of his own experience has coloured the portrait of the second and third servant poems. Yet it is the assurance that the Kingdom is at hand that affects all his words, fills him with joy and creates in him a new song. The strange story of Israel, the meaning of the covenant that was so often betrayed by Israel and renewed by God and the very present humiliation are about to come to the divinely appointed consummation. Presumably this is what is meant by describing this (and other) prophetic words as eschatological – that is teaching about the end of history and the final purpose of God. In the prophets this is often associated with such phrases as 'the Day of the Lord', 'in that day', 'in the days'. But since the word is very difficult to define in a way appropriate to the Old Testament prophets it should be used with hesitation. The prophet's mind is focused on the new thing that God is about to do. This is in contrast with the existing state of affairs. It will bring about a complete change, not only for man but for the natural world. For the prophet there was an intimate relationship between them for good or ill. But it is not suggested that this will take place outside this world or at the end of history. It is rather that history will continue under new conditions, those in which the people of God will come to their divinely appointed maturity, in which therefore all men, and nature itself, will be involved. Thus it is hardly suggested that Israel will engage on a work of world-wide evangelism, but that Israel will be so

manifestly the evidence of the rule of God that she will fulfil
her true priestly task of teaching the ways of God with men.

There are certain distinctive words and phrases in these
chapters to which it is not always possible to give adequate
English equivalents. One of the characteristic phrases which is
shared with the eighth-century prophet is 'the Holy One of
Israel' (twelve times in Isa. 1–39; thirteen times in Isa. 40–66).
So rare is this phrase outside this book as to suggest very
strongly a continuing community of Isaiah's disciples persist-
ing into the exile and beyond. The phrase enshrines a paradox:
he who is unapproachable, wholly other than man and
incalculable, has joined himself to Israel even in Israel's sin
and humiliation. The most distinctive word is, in English,
'ransomer' together with the verb 'ransomed'. Neither this
nor any other English word is adequate to the Hebrew. The
word carries with it the overtones of the nearest relative whose
sacred responsibility it is to come to the help of an impoverished
or enslaved kinsman, or even to avenge one who has been
murdered; cp. Lev. 25: 47–9 ('redeem'); Num. 35: 12 ('next-
of-kin'). This is the theme of the story in the book of Ruth
(Ruth 3: 9, 12 etc., 'next-of-kin'). Together with the description of the LORD as Saviour are the words 'righteous', 'righteousness' and 'justify'. These words have more than a legal
or ethical meaning. They include the victory of right over
wrong, the triumph of the divine purpose, and therefore the
restoration of man to his rightful place within that purpose. ✻

Warnings to keep the moral law

THE RESTORED COMMUNITY

These are the words of the LORD: **56**
Maintain justice, do the right;
for my deliverance is close at hand,

and my righteousness will show itself
　　victorious.

2　Happy is the man who follows these precepts,
　happy the mortal who holds them fast,
　　who keeps the sabbath undefiled,
　who refrains from all wrong-doing!

3　The foreigner who has given his allegiance to the LORD
　　must not say,
　'The LORD will keep me separate from his people for
　　ever';
　　and the eunuch must not say,
　'I am nothing but a barren tree.'

4　For these are the words of the LORD:
　The eunuchs who keep my sabbaths,
　who choose to do my will and hold fast to my covenant,

5　shall receive from me something better than sons and
　　daughters,
　a memorial and a name in my own house and within
　　my walls;
　I will give them*a* an everlasting name,
　a name imperishable for all time.

6　So too with the foreigners who give their allegiance to
　　me, the LORD,
　to minister to me and love my name
　and to become my servants,
　all who keep the sabbath undefiled
　and hold fast to my covenant:

7　them will I bring to my holy hill
　　and give them joy in my house of
　　prayer.

[a] *So Scroll; Heb.* him.

Their offerings and sacrifices shall be acceptable on my
    altar;
    for my house shall be called
    a house of prayer for all nations.
    This is the very word of the Lord GOD,   8
    who brings home the outcasts of Israel:
I will yet bring home all that remain to be brought in.

✱ We can well believe that nothing short of a prophetic
word, introduced by the authoritative 'These are the words
of the LORD' (literally 'Thus has the LORD said'), could have
met the needs of the Jewish community in the years following
the rebuilding of the temple. The hopes aroused in Isa.
40–55, rekindled by Haggai and Zechariah, were completely nullified by the harsh realities of life.

1. Only one who had experienced the prophetic call could
have spoken the closing clauses of verse 1. He is saying 'Prepare yourself by righteous conduct for the revelation of God's
victorious righteousness'.

2 may be seen as a summary of the Law in its ritual (*sabbath*)
and ethical requirements. From the time of the exile sabbath
observance became the most obvious 'outward and visible
sign' of the Jew.

3–7 introduce a new and revolutionary thought, as challeng-
ing as that which faced and threatened the early Christian
community; cp. Acts 10 and 15. It is in flat contradiction
of the law of Deut. 23: 1–6. It is true that Second Isaiah (45:
23f.) had looked for the conversion of the Gentiles; but when
this was translated into practical reality such as conversion of
the pagan officials, it was difficult for the devout Jew to accept.
In the oriental world court officials were often eunuchs. The
reference here, and to foreigners, may suggest, as certainly
happened in the Roman Empire, that the quality of Judaism
after the exile was beginning to attract attention from the
pagan world (cp. Zech. 8: 20–3; Mal. 1: 11). In this passage

the prophet has explicitly taken an all-important step. Loyalty to the covenant outweighs all other considerations. To belong to the people of God depends not at all on physical descent whether of ancestry or descendants. This is the logical consequence of faith in the uniqueness of God, who must be therefore the God of every man, whose temple is primarily *a house of prayer for all nations* rather than a national shrine.

8. It is clear that there are many who have not yet returned from exile. Subsequent history showed that the non-Palestinian Jews were to be an influential factor in shaping Judaism. ✳

CORRUPT LEADERS UNDER JUDGEMENT

9 Come, beasts of the plain, beasts of the forest,
         come, eat your fill,
10 for Israel's watchmen are blind, all of them unaware.
   They are all dumb dogs who cannot bark,
         stretched on the ground, dreaming, lovers of sleep,
11 greedy dogs that can never have enough.
   They are shepherds who understand nothing,
         absent each of them on his own pursuits,
         each intent on his own gain wherever he can find it.
12 'Come,' says each of them, 'let me fetch wine,
         strong, drink and we will drain it down;
      let us make tomorrow like today,
      or greater far!'
57   The righteous perish,
      and no one takes it to heart;
   men of good faith are swept away, but no one cares,
   the righteous are swept away before the onset of evil,
2   but they enter into peace;
      they have run a straight course
      and rest in their last beds.

Come, stand forth, you sons of a soothsayer. 3
You spawn of an adulterer and a harlot,[a]
   who is the target of your jests? 4
  Against whom do you open your mouths
   and wag your tongues,
children of sin that you are, spawn of a lie,
  burning with lust under the terebinths, 5
   under every spreading tree,
  and sacrificing children in the gorges,
   under the rocky clefts?
  And you, woman, 6
  your place is with the creatures of the gorge;
   that is where you belong.
  To them you have dared to pour a libation
   and present an offering of grain.[b]
  On a high mountain-top 7
   you have made your bed;
  there too you have gone up to offer sacrifice.
  In spite of all this am I to relent?[c]
Beside door and door-post you have put up your sign. 8
  Deserting me, you have stripped and lain down[d]
   on the wide bed which you have made,
  and you drove bargains with men
   for the pleasure of sleeping together,
  and you have committed countless acts of fornication[e]
   in the heat of your lust.[f]

[a] and a harlot: *so Sept.; Heb.* and she played the harlot.
[b] *See note on verse 7.*
[c] *Line transposed from end of verse 6.*
[d] lain down: *lit.* gone up.
[e] and you have committed...fornication: *so Sept.; Heb. om.*
[f] in the heat of your lust: *Heb. words of uncertain mng.*

135

9   You drenched your tresses in oil
        blended with many perfumes;
     you sent out your procurers far and wide
        even down to the gates of Sheol.
10   Worn out by your unending excesses,
        even so you never said, 'I am past hope.'
     You earned a livelihood
        and so you had no anxiety.
11   Whom do you fear so much, that you should be false,
     that you never remembered me or gave me[a] a thought?
     Did I not hold my peace and seem not to see
        while you showed no fear of me?
12   Now I will denounce your conduct
        that you think so righteous.
13   These idols of yours shall not help when you cry;
        no idol shall save you.
     The wind shall carry them off, one and all,
        a puff of air shall blow them away;
     but he who makes me his refuge shall possess the earth
        and inherit my holy hill.

✳ As the N.E.B. footnotes suggest, translation and therefore
interpretation of this passage are at times uncertain. But there
is no mistaking the basic meaning of the passage. The leaders
in this society are incapable of fulfilling their proper function,
and their inadequacy stems from their greed and self-indul-
gence. The leaders in religion are also to blame for their
abandonment of Israel's true worship and their indulgence
in the orgiastic practices of Canaanite religion. There is much
in this section which recalls the language of the eighth-century
prophets. Some commentators would regard it as a collection

[a] me: *or, with Scroll,* these things.

136

of oracles from that period preserved among the continuing body of Isaiah's disciples. However, the practices of nature-religion tend to persist long after they have been officially repudiated, as Ezekiel well knew (Ezek. 8). If then the words are addressed to the community after the exile, it is probable that they describe the conduct of the self-appointed leaders, civil and religious, from the ranks of those who had remained in Judaea; those who returned from Babylon were a small minority, and it is improbable that they would so soon have adopted the practices of 57: 5-10.

9. *beasts:* this would be an appropriate metaphor for marauding bands.

10. *watchmen:* a word used by Ezekiel to describe the work of a prophet, but here like 'shepherds' (verse 11) referring to the leaders whose proper business was to guard the integrity of this little province. Instead they were using their position only to profit themselves. The charge against them is that they are incapable, indolent, self-indulgent and utterly selfish.

12 sounds like a drinking song.

57: 1-2. There is some connection between these verses and Ps. 12: 1 and Mic. 7: 2. It is curious that *the righteous* (twice) is singular while *men of good faith* is plural; *they enter* renders a singular verb, as does *they have run*; *last* is an insertion by the N.E.B. before *beds* which may be justified by Ezek. 32: 25 ('resting-place'). Further, the N.E.B. has altered the order of the Hebrew clauses and created the general impression that the righteous, though ill-treated in this life, have at last found a welcome release in death (cp. Job 3: 13-19). But it must be admitted that the Hebrew word for *peace* properly has the meaning of welfare, prosperity, security, and hardly suits a condition of death. It would seem that we have here a quotation from some wisdom saying, summarizing the belief that the righteous man, in spite of present affliction at the hands of the wicked, will eventually receive his reward from God; cp. Ps. 37: 8-11, 37-40. This theme, in terms of immortality for the righteous, is developed in Wisd. of

Sol. 3: 1–9. (It may be noted that all the versions, ancient and modern, have found difficulty with this passage.)

The remainder of the chapter may best be understood as a judgement scene in which those who are promoting a debased religion are summoned (verse 3), charged with their crime (verses 4–11) and judged (verses 12–13). Even here, the concluding sentence of verse 13 contains a promise to the faithful in the language of the Wisdom Psalms (cp. Ps. 37: 9, 11). The vigorous language with which this section opens reflects the horror and disgust of the true worshipper of Yahweh at those who have forsaken Israel's God. Throughout the Old Testament the strongest condemnation is expressed for those who have forsaken the light they had (cp. also Heb. 10: 26–9; 12: 25). The prophet may be saying that those he is addressing are true descendants of their forefathers before the exile, but more probably he is accusing a particular section of people after the exile. He makes the point that their relapse into nature worship is not merely foolish and pointless; it is an offence against the majesty of God, and can only lead to destruction, in which their idols, and those who cling to them, will be blown away like a mirage before a cool breeze.

3f. The gestures are gestures of contempt; perhaps originally against the prophet, but that means they are against Yahweh who has sent him.

5f. These are fertility rites whose sexual acts were understood to transfer to the land the divine potency. Child sacrifice was rare, usually offered in emergency situations; cp. 2 Kings 3: 27. What particular rites were offered in the *gorges* and *rocky clefts* are not known. Since the *creatures* (verse 6) were apparently smooth, as the Hebrew word suggests, some serpent cult may be indicated. (Some would translate 'among the smooth stones of the gorge'; cp. the Revised Standard Version.) In Hebrew there is a play on the words *creatures* and *belong*: these sinuous snakes are the objects of your sinful worship.

7f. The orgiastic nature of the cults is further described

138

here where the word for *sign* apparently indicates some sexual representation as a symbol of fertility (so also verse 10 'a livelihood' where the same word occurs in Hebrew and the clause could be translated 'you found the life of your *sign* (symbol)'; cp. the Revised Standard Version). If this interpretation is correct, then their conduct was particularly obnoxious, since Deuteronomy had required the fixing of a sign on the door-posts as a memorial of their relationship with God.

9. *You drenched your tresses* supposes an emendation, partly suggested by the Vulgate. Alternatively we might translate 'You went down to the King (or Moloch) with oil' understanding it as an appeal to the god of the underworld. This would be consistent with the last line of the verse.

11. They have forsaken Israel's God and exhausted the divine forbearance.

12. Now judgement must be pronounced. What they think to be righteous will be exposed as apostasy. The worst thing in all the world is bad religion.   *

HOPE FOR THE OPPRESSED

Then a voice shall be heard: 14
Build up a highway, build it and clear the track,
  sweep away all that blocks my people's path.
Thus speaks the high and exalted one,   15
whose name is holy, who lives for ever:
  I dwell in a high and holy place
    with him who is broken and humble in spirit,
    to revive the spirit of the humble,
    to revive the courage of the broken.
  I will not be always accusing,   16
  I will not continually nurse my wrath.
  For a breath of life passed out from me,

and by my own act I created living creatures.

17   For a time I was angry at the guilt of Israel;[a]
I smote him in my anger and withdrew my
      favour.
But he ran wild and went his wilful way.

18   Then I considered his ways,
I cured him and gave him relief,
and I brought him comfort in full measure,

19   brought peace to those who mourned for him,
by the words that issue from my lips,
peace for all men, both near and far,
and so I cured him, says the LORD.

20   But the wicked are like a troubled sea,
a sea that cannot rest,
whose troubled waters cast up mud and filth.

21   There is no peace for the wicked,
says the LORD.

✷ It is evident that these words were spoken to those who had
heard the message of Second Isaiah, but are depressed and
bewildered by its non-fulfilment. This message, then, begins
with an obvious allusion to 40: 3f., but now the 'highway'
is understood figuratively. The obstacles to a full realization
of salvation are the lack of faith and hope. This is repeated in
62: 10. Therefore the words of the eighth-century prophet
(Isa. 6: 1–3) and of the Psalms (Ps. 113: 4–7) are recalled. As
though to answer the despairing cry, 'Is God's wrath unending?' they are reminded of the words of Ps. 103: 9.
Israel had indeed incurred the just anger of God and had
suffered the consequences of pursuing 'his wilful way' (verse
17). But the Great Physician has come to heal and restore his

[a] For...Israel: *prob. rdg.*, *cp.* Sept.; *Heb.* I was angry at the guilt of his
unjust gain.

people's total well-being ('peace'). The word of salvation ends on a solemn note. There are those who are still opposed to God. They are like the waters of the abyss, hostile to the Creator (cp. 51: 9f.); they will suffer the same fate.

14. *a voice shall be heard:* literally 'and he will say' or 'he was saying'. The ancient versions vary in their understanding. The subject of the verb may be God or Second Isaiah. In any case the language so closely resembles 40: 3f. that it must be a deliberate allusion, but an application to a new situation. Here it is an inward and spiritual preparation.

15. *lives* in English is ambiguous and can mean either 'is alive' or 'lives in'. The Hebrew word is the same as that for *dwell*. Ambiguity could be avoided by rendering 'whose dwelling is for ever'. *broken and humble:* this refers primarily to the conditions in the age after the exile. They were crushed and dispirited by hardship; cp. Hag. 1: 6.

19. *mourned:* probably a ritual mourning accompanied by a fast. The N.E.B. redivides the sentences of verses 18–19 and paraphrases somewhat. *by the words...my lips* is literally 'fruit of the lips' (cp. the Revised Standard Version), a phrase similar to that proposed by some scholars for a difficult expression in Hos. 14: 2 (cp. the N.E.B. footnote there). *near and far:* those around Jerusalem and those in various parts of the world.

20. *a troubled sea*, i.e. the primeval ocean, held in check by Yahweh and ultimately to be done away (Rev. 21: 1). ✲

GENUINE FASTING

Shout aloud without restraint;   **58**
lift up your voice like a trumpet.
Call my people to account for their transgression
    and the house of Jacob for their sins,
although they ask counsel of me day by day   2
    and say they delight in knowing my ways,

although, like nations which have acted rightly
    and not forsaken the just laws of their gods,
they ask me for righteous laws
    and say they delight in approaching God.

3   Why do we fast, if thou dost not see it?
        Why mortify ourselves, if thou payest no heed?
    Since you serve your own interest only on your fast-day
        and make all your men work the harder,
4   since your fasting leads only to wrangling and strife
        and dealing vicious blows with the fist,
        on such a day you are keeping no fast
        that will carry your cry to heaven.
5   Is it a fast like this that I require,
        a day of mortification such as this,
        that a man should bow his head like a bulrush
        and make his bed on sackcloth and ashes?
        Is this what you call a fast,
        a day acceptable to the LORD?
6   Is not this what I require of you as a fast:
        to loose the fetters of injustice,
        to untie the knots of the yoke,
            to snap every yoke
        and set free those who have been crushed?
7   Is it not sharing your food with the hungry,
        taking the homeless poor into your house,
        clothing the naked when you meet them
        and never evading a duty to your kinsfolk?
8   Then shall your light break forth like the dawn
        and soon you will grow healthy like a wound newly
                        healed;

your own righteousness shall be your vanguard
   and the glory of the LORD your rearguard.
Then, if you call, the LORD will answer;   9
   if you cry to him, he will say, 'Here I am.'
If you cease to pervert justice,
to point the accusing finger and lay false charges,
   if you feed the hungry from your own plenty   10
      and satisfy the needs of the wretched,
   then your light will rise like dawn out of darkness
      and your dusk be like noonday;
   the LORD will be your guide continually   11
   and will satisfy your needs in the shimmering heat;
      he will give you strength of limb;
   you will be like a well-watered garden,
like a spring whose waters never fail.
The ancient ruins will be restored by your own kindred   12
   and you will build once more on ancestral
            foundations;
you shall be called Rebuilder of broken walls,
   Restorer of houses in ruins.

If you cease to tread the sabbath underfoot,   13
and keep my holy day free from your own affairs,[a]
if you call the sabbath a day of joy
   and the LORD's holy day a day to be honoured,
   if you honour it by not plying your trade,
   not seeking your own interest
   or attending to your own affairs,
then you shall find your joy in the LORD,   14
   and I will set you riding on the heights of the earth,

[a] and keep...affairs: *so Scroll; Heb.* and do your own affairs on my
holy day.

and your father Jacob's patrimony shall be yours to
enjoy;
the LORD himself has spoken it.

* Except for verses 13–14 this chapter deals with the practice
of fasting as a religious observance. It is remarkable that such a
practice has no place in the Law, apart from a possible reference in connection with the Day of Atonement. Even there
the word 'fast' does not occur but it may be included in the
phrase 'mortify yourselves' (literally 'afflict' or 'humble
yourselves'; Lev. 16: 29, 31) as in 58: 5 'a day of mortifica-
tion'. It is not certain that fasting is specifically meant by
this phrase; it may mean what we generally understand by
self-denial, which might include fasting. There are several
references to fasting in the historical records, normally
associated with mourning and lamenting for either some
public or some private calamity (2 Sam. 1: 12; 12: 16),
present or threatening. There are only three occurrences in
the Psalter, each time in a lament for an individual (Pss. 35:
13; 69: 10; 109: 24). It was a spontaneous expression of grief
and also apparently intended to arouse the divine pity and
compassion. Abstention from food was also practised in
preparation for the receiving of a divine communication
although this is rare in biblical records (Exod. 34: 28; 1 Kings
19: 8). There is no reference to regularly appointed fast days
until after the exile (Zech. 7: 1–14; 8: 18f.) although at the
threat of invasion from the Babylonian army a fast had been
proclaimed (Jer. 36: 9). When such fasts were held, the poems
in the book of Lamentations would have been appropriate
for public use. The association of 'sabbath' with self-mortifica-
tion in Lev. 16: 31 may account for the inclusion of verses
13–14 in this chapter, which otherwise seem to be unrelated.
The contents of this chapter may have their origin in more
than one occasion but are gathered together because they are
united by a common theme.

The prophet is summoned to address a congregation assembled on a solemn fast day. There is a note of urgency in the opening words, especially in the words 'like a trumpet' (literally ram's horn), for this instrument was used to summon the people to a holy war, or to announce the beginning of a solemn day of worship (Ps. 81: 3). The congregation is in great danger, not from some external foe, but because they are confessedly approaching God, yet in a condition of rebellion ('transgression') against God. The language of verse 2 is particularly emphatic: 'It is I from whom they seek a response as though they were a people in a right relationship with God, yet they have abandoned what I have clearly declared to be my will. To pretend that they wish to know God's will, and come near to him, is worse than frivolous: it is perilous in the extreme.' Verses 3–5 spell this out in detail. There was indeed good reason for a fast day. The returning exiles had been liberated as their prophet (Isa. 40–55) had declared. But it was to conditions of poverty and great hardship. They might well seek God's help and pity. But what was the obstacle to their receiving God's help? Was it not their own lack of real piety? Some of them had leisure to fast; but they saw to it that their fields were not left uncultivated. Instead of strengthening the community they quarrelled among themselves. No doubt they performed all the ritual acts correctly, but these are an empty show when true humility is absent.

In verses 6–7 the tone changes. The pronouns 'you' and 'your' are now singular, whereas in verses 1–5 they are plural. It suggests that those who heard the prophetic word of judgement have been quickened to penitence, and a real unity has been created. They can now hear what the LORD requires (cp. Mic. 6: 8). There is much in these verses, notably in verse 7, that is clearly echoed in Matt. 25: 35f., as also in Israel's Wisdom teaching (cp. Job 31: 16–21). In verse 8 the words of promise are a deliberate allusion to 52: 12, but applied to a new situation. We might even understand 'your own righteousness' not as a modification of that verse but as 'God' who is Israel's righteousness (cp. Jer. 33: 16). This would be a good parallel to 'the glory of the LORD', a phrase signifying the manifestation of the divine presence (cp. Isa. 6: 3). In verse 9 the prophet gives the assurance that when they 'ask counsel' and approach God (verse 2) in the right spirit, he will be present and enter into an intimate relationship with them.

1. *transgression:* the exact meaning of the Hebrew is 'rebellion' and that meaning should be preserved here. The people are in revolt against God.

2. *ask counsel:* this is a technical term for 'seeking' a divine response, whether by a priest or prophet or, as here, by prayer. *nations:* the Hebrew word is singular ('a nation' or 'this nation'). It may be used collectively as in the N.E.B. and so refer to foreign nations in contrast to Israel; or it may be a satirical reference to the nation Israel which ought to have performed the righteous requirements of God.

3. *only:* to avoid ambiguity it might be better to transfer this word to precede *your own interest. make...work the harder:* the verb carries overtones of slave-driving, especially in the context of the Egyptian oppressors (Exod. 3: 7).

8. *vanguard...rearguard:* an allusion to 52: 12.

The second promise is given in verses 9*b*–12, beginning with 'If you cease...'. This may have been given on another but similar occasion and appropriately added here. There is no reference to fasting, and the conditions are of a more general character, resembling Pss. 15: 2–5; 24: 4–6. They may be a reminder of what is really required of those who will come to the rebuilt temple. Without a just ordering of society and a practical concern for the needy, the hopes engendered by Second Isaiah cannot be realized. But when this happens, the prophet is so confident of the divine blessing that he can only express this confidence in a mixture of metaphors: light, sure guidance, abundance of food and water, restoration of health and vigour so that Jerusalem can become once more an inhabited city. As often in such a promise, a new name is given, signifying a new character (cp. 62: 4).

10. *from your own plenty:* this could be translated 'from what you want for yourself'.

13–14. This may be an independent poem, added here because the fasting took place on a sabbath. It refers specifically to Exod. 20: 8–11. It adds a new and positive understanding of the sabbath. It is to be 'a day of joy', as it might well be for those who saw their liberation from Babylon in the light of the deuteronomic explanation of sabbath (Deut. 5: 15). To this day the prayers associated with the sabbath among Jews are full of this note of joy.

14. *riding on the heights of the earth* (cp. Deut. 32: 13). The phrase, originally derived from a Canaanite liturgy, had become a conventional one to indicate sovereignty. In true worship man becomes supreme, whatever be the limitations of his daily existence. He is at one with God, the King of the universe, and enters fully into the ancient promise of God to his people. ✳

WHY DOES NOT GOD HELP?

The LORD's arm is not so short that he cannot save **59**
   nor his ear too dull to hear;
  it is your iniquities that raise a barrier **2**
   between you and your God,
  because of your sins he has hidden his face
   so that he does not hear you.
Your hands are stained with blood
   and your fingers with crime; **3**
your lips speak lies
and your tongues utter injustice.
No man sues with just cause,
  no man goes honestly to law; **4**

all trust in empty words, all tell lies,
conceive mischief and give birth to trouble.

5 They hatch snakes'*^a* eggs, they weave cobwebs;
eat their eggs and you will die,
for rotten eggs hatch only rottenness.

6 As for their webs, they will never make cloth,
no one can use them for clothing;
their works breed trouble
and their hands are busy with deeds of violence.

7 They rush headlong into crime
in furious haste to shed innocent blood;
their schemes are schemes of mischief
and leave a trail of ruin and devastation.

8 They do not know the way to peace,
no justice guides their steps;
all the paths they follow are crooked;
no one who walks in them enjoys true peace.

9 Therefore justice is far away from us,
right does not reach us;
we look for light but all is darkness,
for the light of dawn, but we walk in deep gloom.

10 We grope like blind men along a wall,
feeling our way like men without eyes;
we stumble at noonday as if it were twilight,
like dead men in the ghostly underworld.*^b*

11 We growl like bears,
like doves we moan incessantly,
waiting for justice, and there is none;
for deliverance, but it is still far away.

[a] *Lit.* vipers'.
[b] the ghostly underworld: *mng. of Heb. uncertain.*

Our acts of rebellion against thee are past counting   12
and our sins bear witness against us;
we remember our many rebellions, we know well our
        guilt:
we have rebelled and broken faith with the LORD,   13
we have relapsed and forsaken our God;
we have conceived lies in our hearts and repeated them
in slanderous and treacherous words.
Justice is rebuffed and flouted   14
while righteousness stands aloof;
truth stumbles in the market-place
and honesty is kept out of court,
so truth is lost to sight,   15
and whoever shuns evil is thought a madman.

The LORD saw, and in his eyes it was an evil thing,
      that there was no justice;
he saw that there was no man to help   16
and was outraged that no one intervened;
so his own arm brought him victory
and his own integrity upheld him.
He put on integrity as a coat of mail   17
and the helmet of salvation on his head;
he put on garments of vengeance
and wrapped himself in a cloak of jealous anger.
High God of retribution that he is,   18
he pays in full measure,
wreaking his anger on his foes, retribution on his
      enemies.[a]
So from the west men shall fear his name,   19
fear his glory from the rising of the sun;

[a] *So Sept.; Heb. adds* to coasts and islands he pays in full measure.

for it shall come like a shining river,
the spirit of the LORD hovering over it,
20   come as the ransomer of Zion
and of all in Jacob who repent of their rebellion.
This is the very word of the LORD.

21   This, says the LORD, is my covenant, which I make with
them: My spirit which rests on you and my words which
I have put into your mouth shall never fail you from
generation to generation of your descendants from now
onward for ever. The LORD has said it.

✶ This chapter, with the exception of verse 21, is a unity. It
has been described as a prophetic liturgy similar to Isa. 24–7,
in which prophetic word and community response are inter-
woven. Perhaps a better description would be a prophetic
sermon, introduced by a word of God received by the prophet
(verses 1–3) which he himself develops (verses 4–8). He then
utters in the name of the sinful community a lament leading
to a confession (verses 9–15a). This searching confession
led by the prophet makes it possible for the community
to recognize that God was at work in this evil
situation (verses 15b–20). Like a mighty warrior, but
needing no army, he is about to act, and in ways far beyond
expectation.
     The divisions are clearly defined in the N.E.B. and can be
recognized by the change of pronouns, 'your', 'they', 'we',
'his' (i.e. God's). It is reasonable to suppose that this section
was spoken to the community gathered for a solemn assembly,
in which the words of the psalms were chanted (e.g. Ps. 89:
10, 13). This only served to sharpen the distress and bewilder-
ment of the worshippers. They would remember the words of
Second Isaiah (50: 2) and would say: 'But God has not
fulfilled his promise.' We need to recognize, as throughout chs.
56–66, the pitiable conditions to which the exiles had returned.

1. The returned exiles began to think that God was either impotent (his arm was too short) or indifferent (*his ear too dull*).

2. To this the prophet's word is immediate and vigorous. 'By your conduct you have separated yourselves [N.E.B. *raise a barrier*] from God'; the same word is used in Lev. 11: 47, 'make a distinction'.

3. He reminds them of Isaiah's words in 1: 15. The language of this verse is developed in precise terms in verse 7. The reference to *Your hands* and *your fingers* is pointed, since in the prayers the hands were outstretched as though to receive God's gifts. The Christian parallel would be the position of the hands at the rail in the Communion service.

4. The *lies* etc. refer to false witness, and decisions in the law courts turning justice, which ought to preserve society, into a mockery.

5–6. Apparently the vivid expressions at the end of verse 4 gave rise to the metaphors in these verses. The result of their conduct is to poison the life of society and to rob the people of all protection. A society which allows such perversion of justice can never know that health and vigour ('peace', verse 8) which is the divine purpose for man.

9–11. The prophetic exhortation issues in a lament and confession of sin. He leads the congregation in this act of contrition with the expectation that his own inspired understanding of the fearful truth and his repentance will penetrate into the lives and thoughts of the congregation. This is an important aspect of the prophetic experience. However vigorously he must judge his people for their acts of rebellion, they are still God's people, of whom he is one (cp. 6: 5). The *justice* and *right* of verse 9 are the divine requirements for man's true living, and the divine triumph over all that destroys or constricts human life. The words are an alternative form of the lament presupposed in verse 1. They are followed by a recollection of the curse in Deut. 28: 29 (cp. Amos 5: 18–20). The strange similes in verse 11 apparently mean that while they had been behaving like savage beasts (see verse 7) now they are moaning *like doves*.

12–15a. At last the truth becomes clear and a humble confession is made. The repetition of *rebellion* in these verses draws attention to God as King, and therefore to the seriousness of breaking faith. Characteristically this is expressed in terms of the corruption of human relationships. As the prophet saw it, the breakdown of social justice was an inevitable consequence of the lack of faithfulness (truth) to the covenant God.

16. *no one intervened*. It is apparent that the main charge was against the leaders of the community. *intervened* is the same word as that in 53: 12 'interceded'. Intercession commonly appears in the Old Testament as a function of the prophet. This may have been partly due to the failure of the king as the LORD's anointed to fulfil his proper function as intercessor, and it may be to the absence of a Davidic ruler that this verse refers. God is described as 'appalled' (*was outraged*). For *victory* read 'deliverance' and for *integrity* 'victorious purpose'. This is the God of battles still, though the enemies may be moral and spiritual evils (cp. Wisd. of Sol. 5: 17–23; Eph. 6: 14–17).

17. *vengeance* is too negative a word in English; 'vindication' might be better. It includes the punishment of evil-doers, but is primarily designed to promote righteousness, and so forms an essential element in the fulfilment of God's rule (Luke 18: 7). Similarly, *jealous anger* may mislead. The Hebrew has no word for anger. The divine 'jealousy' is God's ardent zeal for the loyal, and against the rebellious.

18. The text of this verse is uncertain, although the general meaning is clear. We should not forget that retribution has a positive as well as a negative meaning: God holds the scales of justice. There is no word for *wreaking* in the Hebrew. What is meant is that those who oppose the righteous purpose of the divine King will meet his wrath and requital for their rebellions. Further it should be recalled that what we render by

abstract nouns, Hebrew represented as the personal reaction of a personal God; cp. Rom. 2: 5–10. What is described in verses 16–20 is a self-manifestation of God at the end of the age, which will be universal in its scope, generating awe and reverence in all. It is striking that what was described in 8: 7–8 as a terrifying occasion of fear is now (verses 19–20) an effective power for salvation.

21. This is probably a later addition, but it is a fitting conclusion to what has been said in chs. 56–9. It reads like a collection of words of promise (cp. 2 Sam. 23: 2; Isa. 51: 16; Ezek. 36: 26–7) reaffirmed for the renewed and restored people of God. ✳

Promise of the new Jerusalem

✳ A number of poems, closely related in theme and spirit, open the next part of the book and cover chs. 60–2. They are concerned to proclaim that the people's deliverance has come. Taken together they approximate very closely to the language and message of Isa. 40–55: some would therefore regard them as coming from that prophet. There are a few indications that they were spoken in Judaea after the return under Sheshbazzar or even Zerubbabel, but they are slight. If therefore we treat these chapters as composed early after the exile this must be regarded as probable rather than certain. The temple seems to have been rebuilt though sparsely furnished (cp. 60: 7; 62: 9), but the walls of Jerusalem have not been rebuilt (60: 10; 61: 4). It is evident that the great expectations of Second Isaiah have not been realized (for reasons indicated in chs. 56–9) and his word needs to be reaffirmed. Chs. 56–9 and chs. 60–2 are closely related in thought, so that, although the N.E.B. provides a new heading between them, both sections are based on the theme of deliverance. In chs. 60–2 the prophet thinks of a new kind of

deliverance, a deliverance from weakness of morale and
disillusionment in order to prepare for the coming of the
kingdom of God. ✻

THE NEW JERUSALEM

60   Arise, Jerusalem,*a*
            rise clothed in light; your light has come
              and the glory of the LORD shines over you.
2   For, though darkness covers the earth
                and dark night the nations,
              the LORD shall shine upon you
              and over you shall his glory appear;
3   and the nations shall march towards your light
                and their kings to your sunrise.

4   Lift up your eyes and look all around:
              they flock together, all of them, and come to you;
            your sons also shall come from afar,
            your daughters walking beside them leading the way.
5   Then shall you see, and shine with joy,
              then your heart shall thrill with pride:*b*
            the riches of the sea shall be lavished upon you
            and you shall possess the wealth of nations.

6   Camels in droves shall cover the land,
                dromedaries of Midian and Ephah,
            all coming from Sheba
            laden with golden spice*c* and frankincense,
              heralds of the LORD's praise.
7   All Kedar's flocks shall be gathered for you,
              rams of Nebaioth shall serve your need,

[a] Jerusalem: *so Sept.; Heb. om.*   [b] *So some MSS.; others* relief.
[c] golden spice: *or* gold.

    acceptable offerings on my altar,
    and glory shall be added*a* to glory in my temple.

    Who are these that sail along like clouds,   8
       that fly like doves to their dovecotes?
   They are vessels assembling from the coasts and islands, 9
       ships from Tarshish leading the convoy;
    they bring your sons from afar,
    their gold and their silver with them,
       to the honour of the Lord your God,
       the Holy One of Israel;
       for he has made you glorious.

    Foreigners shall rebuild your walls   10
       and their kings shall be your servants;
       for though in my wrath I struck you down,
       now I have shown you pity and favour.
    Your gates shall be open continually,   11
    they shall never be shut day or night,
    that through them may be brought the wealth of
       nations
       and their kings under escort.

  For the nation or kingdom which refuses to serve you 12
shall perish, and wide regions shall be laid utterly waste.

    The wealth of Lebanon shall come to you,   13
   pine, fir,*b* and boxwood,*c* all together,
       to bring glory to my holy sanctuary,
       to honour the place where my feet rest.
   The sons of your oppressors shall come forward to do 14
       homage,

[a] shall be added: *so Sept.; Heb.* I will add.
[b] *Or* elm. [c] *Or* cypress.

all who reviled you shall bow low at your feet;
> they shall call you the City of the LORD,
>> the Zion of the Holy One of Israel.

15   No longer will you be deserted,
> a wife hated and unvisited;^a
> I will make you an eternal pride
> and a never-ending joy.

16   You shall suck the milk of nations
> and be suckled at the breasts of kings.

So you shall know that I the LORD am your deliverer,
> your ransomer the Mighty One of Jacob.

17   For bronze^b I will bring you gold
> and for iron I will bring silver,

bronze^b for timber and iron for stone;
> and I will make your government be peace
> and righteousness rule over you.

18   The sound of violence shall be heard no longer in your
land,
> or ruin and devastation within your borders;
> but you shall call your walls Deliverance
> and your gates Praise.

19   The sun shall no longer be your light by day,
> nor the moon shine on you when evening falls;^c
> the LORD shall be your everlasting light,
> your God shall be your glory.

20   Never again shall your sun set
> nor your moon withdraw her light;

[a] *Or* divorced and unmated.
[b] *Or* copper.
[c] when evening falls: *prob. rdg., cp. Scroll; Heb. obscure in context.*

but the LORD shall be your everlasting light
   and the days of your mourning shall be ended.

Your people shall all be righteous   21
and shall for ever possess the land,
   a shoot of my own planting,
a work of my own hands to bring me glory.
The few shall become ten thousand,   22
   the little nation great.
   I am the LORD;
soon, in the fullness of time, I will bring this to pass.

✶ This chapter may well be described as an application of 49:
7–26 to the circumstances of the early period after the exile.
For all its superlative beauty, it might be dismissed as little
better than a dream, but for its magnetic effect on Jewish and
Christian thought. We may say that no temple such as this,
not Zerubbabel's or even Herod's, was ever built. But the
prophet is looking to the New Age, that goal of all human
history which for him is the supreme reality because it is
God's purpose. This is no earthly temple, but it is that divine
temple to which every earthly temple points. Similarly
Jerusalem never at any time reached this magnificence.
Indeed until at least sixty years later (Nehemiah's day) it
remained a sparsely inhabited place, lacking even a wall,
without which it could hardly be a city (Neh. 2: 3–5, 17).
What is envisaged is some miraculous work of God which will
transform the miserable ruin into a glorious city of God.

   While the poem is a unity (with the possible exception of
verse 12 in prose) the divisions indicated in the N.E.B. may
be treated as stanzas of varying length and theme. The changes
of pronoun should be noted: God is spoken of in the third
person in verses 1–3, 6, 8–9 and 19–20 (and probably verses
4–5 should be included), but speaks directly in the first person
in the remaining verses concluding with the solemn words

at the end of verse 22. The distinction between the third- and
first-person stanzas is not great; the former may indicate
man's response to the divine self-manifestation in the latter.

1-3. The breaking of the dawn. While the valley is still
shrouded in darkness the first rays of the sun light up the city
on Mt Zion. This is what it will be like for all mankind as the
divine *glory*, God's majestic presence, is seen over Zion. It
becomes the focal point for mankind's longing for salvation.
There seems to be a deliberate allusion to 9: 2 and perhaps also
to Gen. 1: 3 and Exod. 10: 21-3; the language forms part of
the background to John 1: 4-18. Verse 3 seems to describe a
religious procession.

4-5. First *all* the exiles, not merely that devoted few who in
fact came, will return, bringing with them the *wealth of
nations* among whom they had been living. *thrill with pride:*
this may be a correct understanding of the unusual Hebrew.
It could also mean 'tremble' (before the immensity of the
revelation) and 'stretch your mind' (to comprehend it).

6-7. This stanza continues with the familiar language
describing the merchant tribes east of Palestine. First they will
bring the good news (*heralds*) of God's saving words which
evoke *praise*, then they provide the sacrificial offerings. All
this is not to foster national pride but to give glory to God.
(Verb and noun for *glory* occur six times in this chapter.)

8-9 continue by referring to the merchants of the Mediterranean; cp. 43: 5. Unless this is the language of hyperbole,
it suggests a wider 'dispersion' of Jews than one would expect
at this period. It is possible that verses 4-9 mean no more than
'by land and sea'.

10-11. From here until verse 18 God speaks directly
through his prophet's lips. What is now being described is the
rebuilding of Jerusalem. The city which foreigners destroyed
will be by *Foreigners* rebuilt, for God who ordered the one
orders the other. The point of verse 11 would be clear to the
ancient world; the city gates would normally be closed as a
protection against marauders. In the New Age this will be

unnecessary in a time of security, and even more because of the never-ending flow of wealth.

12. This verse is in prose. It may be a scribe's comment originally in the margin and later included in the text. It is certainly inappropriate in this context.

13–14. The magnificent trees of Lebanon will be used as timber for adorning the temple, as they were for Solomon's building. Again the *homage* of the *oppressors* is to do honour to God, not Israel. Throughout this chapter the second person pronoun is feminine singular, and this is precisely defined in verse 14 as *City of the LORD* and *Zion of the Holy One of Israel*. What is meant is not the political city of Jerusalem, but that place to which Israel gathered to worship, the place of the *holy sanctuary* (cp. Ezek. 48: 35).

15–16. The promise of 54: 6f. is renewed. Zion, once deserted, will be restored to its early place in Israel's worship. The grief of Lam. 2: 15 will be reversed. It may be noted that the particular word for *joy* occurs more frequently in these chapters of Isaiah than in any other book of the Old Testament, but in Ps. 48: 2 Mt Zion is described as 'the joy of the whole earth'.

17–18. A description of the New Age which will be all that Solomon's should have been; cp. 1 Kings 10: 14–22. Alien rule (i.e. Persian) will be replaced by *peace* and *righteousness*, and the walls of Jerusalem will be rebuilt and become (*you shall call...*) what they had failed to be in the past, *Deliverance* and *Praise* to God.

19–20. In these verses the prophet himself reflects on his oracle in verses 1–3. If *the LORD shall be your everlasting light* there is no need for sun and moon, but the new creation is a fulfilment of the first, not its repudiation. This passage is quoted in Rev. 21: 23.

21–2. A final affirmation with the solemn words *I am the LORD*. The promise to Abraham will be fulfilled in the New Age, when his true descendants will conform to God's purpose (*be righteous*). All opposition to God, and unwillingness

to do his will, will disappear, and the people of God *shall...
possess the land* (cp. Gen. 15: 18). ✳

THE YEAR OF THE LORD'S FAVOUR

61   The spirit of the Lord GOD is upon me
        because the LORD has anointed me;
        he has sent me to bring good news to the humble,
            to bind up the broken-hearted,
        to proclaim liberty to captives
            and release to those in prison;[a]
2   to proclaim a year of the LORD's favour
            and a day of the vengeance of our God;
        to comfort all who mourn,[b]
3   to give them garlands instead of ashes,
            oil of gladness instead of mourners' tears,
            a garment of splendour for the heavy heart.
        They shall be called Trees of Righteousness,
            planted by the LORD for his glory.
4   Ancient ruins shall be rebuilt
            and sites long desolate restored;
            they shall repair the ruined cities
            and restore[c] what has long lain desolate.
5   Foreigners shall serve as shepherds of your flocks,
            and aliens shall till your land and tend your vines;
6   but you shall be called priests of the LORD
            and be named ministers of our God;
            you shall enjoy the wealth of other nations
            and be furnished[d] with their riches.

[a] release to those in prison: *or, with Sept.*, sight to the blind.
[b] *Prob. rdg.; Heb. adds* to appoint to Zion's mourners.
[c] restore: *so Scroll; Heb. om.*
[d] be furnished: *prob. rdg.; Heb. unintelligible.*

And so, because shame in double measure   7
  and jeers and insults*ᵃ* have been my people's*ᵇ* lot,
they shall receive in their own land a double measure
          of wealth,
  and everlasting joy shall be theirs.
For I, the LORD, love justice   8
  and hate robbery and wrong-doing;
I will grant them a sure reward
  and make an everlasting covenant with them;
  their posterity will be renowned among the   9
          nations
    and their offspring among the peoples;
  all who see them will acknowledge in them
a race whom the LORD has blessed.

Let me rejoice in the LORD with all my heart,   10
  let me exult in my God;
  for he has robed me in salvation as a garment
    and clothed me in integrity as a cloak,
like a bridegroom with his priestly garland,
  or a bride decked in her jewels.
  For, as the earth puts forth her blossom   11
  or bushes in the garden burst into flower,
so shall the Lord GOD make righteousness and praise
  blossom before all the nations.

✷ In general terms this chapter may be seen as a development
of the message in ch. 60, but the development is of a highly
distinctive character. The opening words (perhaps extending
to verse 4) have many features that resemble the Servant

[a] and insults: *prob. rdg.; Heb.* they shout in triumph.
[b] my people's: *lit.* their.

Poems, especially 42: 1–4; 49: 1–6, and so some would regard 61: 1–3 (4) as a further Servant Poem. It is perhaps better to regard these verses as deliberately modelled on the earlier poems. But the further development in verses 5–9 is no less striking. It clearly envisages a fulfilment of the ancient covenant word in Exod. 19: 5–6 which declared Israel's priestly function for the nations. We should note that the language of verses 1–2 ('to proclaim') suggests some kind of connection of thought with the Year of Jubilee (Lev. 25: 8–55). The heart of the chapter is verses 5–9, to which the call (verses 1–3/4) is the preface, and the hymn (verses 10–11) is the epilogue.

1. The opening lines sound like a call to prophecy, although it must be admitted that *spirit* (except for Ezekiel) and anointing were not normally associated with Judaean prophecy in the days before the exile. Both are aspects of Kingship (2 Sam. 23: 1f.). *he has sent me to bring good news* sounds like the designation of a herald, and this would be appropriate to a prophet; *to proclaim liberty* seems to refer to Lev. 25: 10 where the release of slaves was integral to the Jubilee Year. The full and detailed treatment in Lev. 25 is important. It is obvious that it could never have been fully put into practice, and it may be argued that the detailed statement arose among the exiled priests. Yet they could hardly have invented the Year of Jubilee with its solemn act of liberation for slaves. (About fifty years later a similar action was demanded by Nehemiah; Neh. 5: 1–13.) We may regard this religious observance as the background to these verses. This passage is quoted by Jesus at the beginning of his ministry in Nazareth (Luke 4: 17–19) and he added that at that point the ancient word had come true. There appears to be some connection between these verses and Ps. 147, a Psalm dating from after the exile, associated with the Feast of Tabernacles. It appears that that message is of such startling character that the messenger must be empowered by God (*The spirit*) and authorized by him (*sent*) to deliver it. *bring*

good news: this includes not only the message but action (*bind up*) and solemn proclamation. It may be said that in these verses all the functions of the LORD's Anointed, disintegrated by the exile, are brought together again in the prophet's vision of the New Age. But who is the royal messenger? It is certainly no individual prophet. It would seem that a number of elements in Second Isaiah's message have been synthesized. If we recall Zion as the bringer of good news (40: 9 footnote), the Servant as Israel, the spirit-filled people of God (42: 1) inheriting the Davidic role (55: 3-4) and therefore, at last, fulfilling the priestly function of instruction in God's requirements (42: 4, 21), the *me* in this passage may well be Zion, the worshipping community of God's people. It is that community that is deeply stirred on behalf of the afflicted, and the imprisoned who must be freed in this 'year of the LORD's favour'.

2. This is the function of the Messianic community. The *day of the vengeance* is the day in which God sets right all that is wrong and perverted in his world (cp. 59: 17). There seems little justification for the suggestion that Jesus did not include this clause in order to avoid the idea of divine 'vengeance', since he includes precisely this in Luke 18: 7-8. The suggestion arises from a modern and non-biblical narrowing of the content of vengeance. Jesus, like any other rabbi, quoted enough to call the whole passage to mind.

3. *garlands instead of ashes* is in Hebrew a skilful play on words in which the same consonants, but in a different order, occur in both words; also the first word would recall the word for *glory* at the end of this verse and in 60: 7, 9, 13. An approximation in English might be 'sashes instead of ashes'. *garment of splendour* is a somewhat free rendering. The Hebrew means 'a song of praise'. The verse closes with a renaming, i.e. the people will be given a new character (cp. 60: 14). It will be evident to all that they are the LORD's people in whom his purpose is triumphant (*Righteousness*).

4. This prophet, like his predecessors, had visions, but he

was no visionary. In quite practical terms, his hope for the future included the rebuilding of devastated towns and villages, apparently by the Jews themselves. The verbs are not passive but third person plural active, 'they shall rebuild' etc.

6. But the restored community shall serve as priests in order to instruct the nations in God's requirements for worship and conduct. It should be recalled that the primary function of priesthood in Israel's early life was to teach the covenant requirements; cp. Deut. 33: 10. Their material support will come from those who had previously ignored or despised them. *ministers:* the Hebrew word, like the English, did not necessarily have a narrow religious significance, but readily acquired it, and is here parallel to *priests*.

8–9. A direct word of God declaring his hostility to all oppression and his activity on behalf of his loyal worshippers. *race* now has overtones which are inappropriate to the original. We should understand the word in the sense in which Paul argues in Rom. 4: 13–22. In much the same way Israel's future is assured not by physical descent, but by the everlasting covenant and the blessing of the God of Abraham.

10–11. The prophet's response in a hymn, whereby he leads the people into the certainty created in him by his call. It would be better to render the opening words 'I will greatly rejoice.' The language is appropriate to a wedding feast: the garments are *salvation* and 'righteousness' or 'victory' (*integrity*). The *priestly garland* was apparently a particular form of headdress similar to that worn by the priest, and worn only at the marriage ceremony. As if to emphasize the certainty of the promises in verses 5–9 whose fulfilment seemed so improbable, the prophet recalls the experience common to those who cultivate the soil. There is both mystery and assurance in the way in which the soil produces the crops; no less mysterious and assured is the fulfilment of the divine purpose for all mankind.   ✳

THE IMPORTUNATE PROPHET

For Zion's sake I will not keep silence, **62**
 for Jerusalem's sake I will speak out,
until her right shines forth like the sunrise,
 her deliverance like a blazing torch,
until the nations see the triumph of your right 2
 and all kings see your glory.
Then you shall be called by a new name
which the LORD shall pronounce with his own lips;
 you will be a glorious crown in the LORD's hand, 3
  a kingly diadem*ᵃ* in the hand of your God.
No more shall men call you Forsaken, 4
no more shall your land be called Desolate,
but you shall be named Hephzi-bah*ᵇ*
 and your land Beulah;*ᶜ*
 for the LORD delights in you
  and to him your land is wedded.
 For, as a young man weds a maiden, 5
  so you shall wed him who rebuilds you,
 and your God shall rejoice over you
  as a bridegroom rejoices over the bride.
I have posted watchmen on your walls, Jerusalem, 6
who shall not keep silence day or night:
 'You who invoke the LORD's name,
take no rest, give him no rest 7
 until he makes Jerusalem
 a theme of endless praise on earth.'

[a] diadem: *lit.* turban.
[b] *That is* My delight is in her.
[c] *That is* Wedded.

8   The LORD has sworn with raised right hand and mighty
            arm:
      Never again will I give your grain to feed your foes
          or let foreigners drink the new wine
              for which you have toiled;
9   but those who bring in the corn shall eat and praise the
            LORD,
      and those who gather the grapes shall drink in my holy
            courts.

10   Go out of the gates, go out,
      prepare a road for my people;
      build a highway, build it up,
          clear away the boulders;
      raise a signal to the peoples.
11   This is the LORD's proclamation
          to earth's farthest bounds:
      Tell the daughter of Zion,
          Behold, your deliverance has come.
          His recompense comes with him;
          he carries his reward before him; ·
12   and they shall be called a Holy People,
          the Ransomed of the LORD,
      a People long-sought, a City not forsaken.

⁎ There is a quality of splendid impatience in this chapter,
an impatience which is uninhibited within the assurance that
God hears and answers. This is a common phenomenon in the
'individual laments' of the Psalter (cp. Pss. 10; 13; note
particularly the concluding verses). Jewish tradition referred
to the Levites as having a particular duty to cry aloud the
words of Ps. 44: 23 ('Bestir thyself, Lord; why dost thou
sleep?'). So here it is the intercessory function of the prophet

that is to the fore. He shares to the full in the distress of his people that the magnificent promises of Second Isaiah have not been fulfilled, and there is no indication that they will be (cp. Zech. 1: 12). But he is confident that this prayer for deliverance will be answered; that is what makes the startling language of verse 7 possible. Once more we hear the words giving to Zion and the people of God 'a new name' (verses 2–4 and 12), i.e. a distinctive and manifest role to play in relation to all mankind. If we feel that the language is extravagant, we should observe the thoroughly practical note sounded in verses 8–9. These verses may indeed give the clue to the living context of this prophetic poem. The exiles have returned, but to a land that is still occupied territory and certainly no garden of Eden (51: 3). They have to pay taxes in kind (62: 8), and there is no evidence at all that the nations will come with splendid gifts. If in verse 9 'my holy courts' indicates the rebuilt temple, then even the hopes engendered by Haggai and Zechariah have proved false. All this gives urgency to the prophetic prayer (verse 1) and to the command given to the watchmen (members of the prophetic community or angelic beings?) in verse 6.

1–2. A prophetic oracle, i.e. one in which the prayer of the people and the divine assurance meet, for the prophet who is the spokesman of God is also the focal point of his people's life. *her right* is parallel to *her deliverance* (verse 1) and means her triumphant restoration (by God) (cp. verse 2 where *triumph of your right* is exactly the same noun). The promise of divine vindication is assured, since the *new name* will be pronounced by God himself.

4. The N.E.B. footnotes should be observed in order to appreciate the development throughout verses 4–5. *is wedded* in the days before the exile was more than a metaphor, for in Canaanite religion the god (Ba'al) fertilized the ground he wedded (*bā'al*) and this was dramatically represented at the high places. But by this time the ancient Semitic myth and ritual had been forgotten, and the language of verse 5 shows

that it is no more than a strongly emotional metaphor drawn from human experience.

6–7. *You who invoke the LORD's name:* this phrase in Hebrew has a much greater significance than the English might suggest. The word for *invoke* is used for one of David's court officials (2 Sam. 8: 16, 'secretary of state'), whose function appears to have been to keep the king constantly informed about events so that he might take appropriate action. This would be a natural mode of thought of the ancient world with its primary concept of God as King, and leads into the following verse, *give him no rest*. It would not have occurred to the Jew that because God knows all, man has no need to pray either for himself or others. The God of Israel is a real person and responds as a person to his people's prayers.

8–9. This is the divine response in the form of a solemn oath. Again the very language of the oath implies that God involves himself wholly in what he utters. We are not told who the *foes* and *foreigners* were. They may have been Edomites, who during this period had occupied much of the territory of southern Judah, or marauding bands from the desert. It is probable, however, that they were tax-collectors appointed by the Persians. These might have been Arabians or Ammonites as in Nehemiah's day (Neh. 2: 19).

10–12. To a large extent the phrases in these verses have been gathered together from Second Isaiah, especially Isa. 40. First they recall the triumphant faith of the prophet of the exile, many of whose predictions have already been fulfilled (Cyrus, Babylon, return from exile), and requicken fading hopes. Secondly, in the post-exile and Judaean setting their original meaning has been changed. They may still refer to Jews in Babylonia (the great majority) who are to return. But the connection with the closing words of verse 9 points to a new application, one related to some celebration in the rebuilt temple. The great stones of the old city wall, pulled down and scattered on the route to the temple, made a

religious procession practically impossible. The processional
highway must be restored to its former condition (Isa. 40: 3),
so that the celebration of the exodus, now given an enriched
meaning, can be fully restored (cp. Isa. 11: 16). This will be
a signal to the peoples (cp. 49: 22) but much more a re-awaken-
ing of the faith of Zion's inhabitants.

12. The bringing together of the various names is a reaffirmation of God's word to his people: *Holy People* (Exod.
19: 6), *Ransomed of the LORD* (Isa. 35: 9-10; cp. Exod. 15:
13), *long-sought* (Ezek. 34: 11), *not forsaken* (Isa. 62: 4). When
the prophet's hearers recall and reflect on these names, they
will know their true place in the Kingdom of God. This is
what 'deliverance' means.   ✳

BEHOLD THE SEVERITY OF GOD

'Who is this coming from Edom,   **63**
coming from Bozrah, his garments stained red?
Under his clothes his muscles stand out,
  and he strides, stooping in his might.'
It is I, who announce that right has won the day,
  I, who am strong to save.
'Why is your clothing all red,   2
like the garments of one who treads grapes in the vat?'
I have trodden the winepress alone;   3
no man, no nation was with me.
  I trod them down in my rage,
  I trampled them in my fury;
and their life-blood spurted over my garments
  and stained all my clothing.
  For I resolved on a day of vengeance;   4
  the year for ransoming my own had come.
  I looked for a helper but found no one,   5

I was amazed that there was no one to support me;
yet my own arm brought me victory,
alone my anger supported me.

6   I stamped on nations in my fury,
          I pierced them in my rage
and let their life-blood run out upon the ground.

* The very real difficulties of this poem for the religious
mind should be neither minimized by any attempt to weaken
the harshness of the language, nor exaggerated by overlooking
the fact that it is poetry, and is using the familiar language of
oriental poetry. Clearly there is a connection of thought with
ch. 34. Again it picks up the words of 59: 15*b*–18. While
it is hardly likely to be the work of the prophet of chs. 60–2
or of 63: 7–19, the compiler of these chapters felt that this
was an appropriate place for the poem. The closing section of
ch. 62 and the rest of ch. 63 form the setting and intended
context for this poem. 'Deliverance has come' for the people
of God, and this is the work of God's 'unfailing love'.
Clearly those who seek to oppose this majestic work of
salvation are bound to bring disaster upon themselves. It is
in the nature of things that the overcoming of evil in individuals as well as in society cannot be achieved without
suffering both by those who seek to overcome evil with good,
and by those who are entrenched in evil. We would express
this in abstract language. Hebrew, with its intense awareness
of a personal God, finds in the language of the battlefield the
only terminology adequate to the age-long struggle between
good and evil.

These verses may best be understood as looking to the End
of the Age, when all opposition to the royal purpose of God
will reach its climax and be finally overcome. In the vivid
language drawn from the psalms (cp. Ps. 68) the prophet
describes the divine intervention. The forces hostile to God are
described as Edom (see comment on verse 1). Clearly this is

not the Edomite people of the days after the exile, since they were themselves a much reduced people, largely forced out of their ancestral territory to find new homes in the southern part of Judah which they occupied as far north as Hebron. This situation seems to lie behind the obscurities of 21: 11–17; Jer. 49: 7–22. There was, however, an ancient rivalry between the Israelite and Edomite peoples, certainly from the time of David (1 Kings 11: 15–18) and thereafter during the monarchy period (cp. Amos 1: 11–12). We can well understand how Edom became a conventional name for the enemies of Israel (Ps. 60: 8–11). This ancient rivalry was deepened during the Babylonian period (Ezek. 35; Lam. 4: 21f.). Of course all this is represented from the Jewish point of view, but the plain fact was that much of the Judaean territory became Edomite, its population either killed or driven out. Thus, much as the word 'vandal', originally a tribal name, has became a descriptive term in English, so for this prophet Edom represents non-Jewish opposition to the LORD. It will be the first to feel the attack on the nations, in the Day of the LORD when all who have been injured and oppressed will be restored to health and freedom (verses 4–5). As the punctuation shows, the poem is presented in the form of a dialogue, the questions by the city's sentinel, the answers by God himself.

1. *Edom...Bozrah:* the similarity in Hebrew to the words for 'red' and 'vintager' would be at once appreciated by the hearers. It points forward to the metaphors of vintage festival in verses 2f. Bozrah was the capital city of Edom. Yahweh's marching from Edom (or Seir) to help his people was part of the conventional picture (cp. Judg. 5: 4). *Under his clothes...:* the picture is difficult in this context. The common translation 'glorious in apparel' (cp. the Revised Standard Version) might be retained. The remainder of the verse is based on a slight emendation but may be confidently accepted (cp. the Revised Standard Version). *right has won the day* or, rather more concretely, 'with (a song of) triumph'; cp. Judg. 5: 11 where the same Hebrew noun is used.

4. *day of vengeance:* better 'a day of vindication for the oppressed'.

5. This verse is practically identical with 59: 16, but is given a new application against 'Edom'.

6. *pierced:* older renderings prefer 'made drunk', an idea associated with the cup of the LORD's wrath (cp. Jer. 25: 15). Some Hebrew manuscripts have a very similar word meaning 'shatter' which is also very appropriate. *

A PRAYER OF SUPPLICATION AND PENITENCE

* Clearly 63: 7 – 64: 12 is not what is normally understood by prophecy. It is a psalm with many parallels in the Psalter (cp. Ps. 44). It may have been composed for some particular historical situation, although the lack of precise historical reference makes it difficult to point to such an occasion. Two passages might be cited as pointing to an event of recent date; 63: 18; 64: 11. The obvious biblical parallels are Lamentations and Pss. 74 and 79. Some have argued for a disaster in the fifth century, i.e. following the rebuilding of the temple, but the evidence for this is tenuous. Those who have lived in places where church buildings have suffered some physical disaster know how the language of prayer relating to such a disaster can persist even after restoration is complete. A modern hymn-book may still include a hymn which runs:

'The fell disease on every side walks forth with tainted breath;
And pestilence, with rapid stride bestrews the land with death'

referring to the plague which was so terrible an experience of earlier centuries, but which may now be given a more general application.

Originally, then, this passage may have been composed in the same period as Lamentations, and in Judaea, but perhaps a little before the oracles of Second Isaiah. The fact that this is a carefully composed prayer with a definite

structure does not preclude the possibility that it is the work
of a prophet. An intercessory prayer occurs in ch. 59. The
intercessory function of the prophet is referred to in biblical
(Jer. 15: 1) and later Jewish literature. It may be difficult to
determine whether the present prayer was composed as a
single poem or whether it has drawn together into a unity
existing prayers. It divides naturally into four main sections:
(a) 63: 7–14, a hymn-like confession of faith, in which is
included a preparation for penitence (verses 10–11a) and
supplication (verses 11b–14); (b) the lament over present
conditions (verses 15–19); (c) a prayer for help (64: 1–7); (d)
a prayer for forgiveness (64: 8–12). The form is that of a
community lament.

The psalm must be read as a unit, but for convenience it is
divided in this commentary into its two main sections: 63:
7–19; 64. It will be observed from the footnotes that the
Hebrew text presents many difficulties of detail, but this does
not affect the main content of the psalm. ✳

I will recount the LORD's acts of unfailing love   7
and the LORD's praises as High God,
all that the LORD has done for us
and his great goodness to the house of Israel,
all that he has done for them in his tenderness
and by his many acts of love.
He said, 'Surely they are my people,   8
my sons who will not play me false';
and he became their deliverer in all their troubles.   9
It was no envoy, no angel, but he himself that delivered
them;
he himself ransomed them by his love and pity,
lifted them up and carried them
through all the years gone by.

10   Yet they rebelled and grieved his holy spirit;
          only then was he changed into their enemy
             and himself fought against them.
11   Then men remembered days long past
          and him who drew out*[a]* his people:*[b]*
       Where is he who brought them up from the Nile*[c]*
          with the shepherd*[d]* of his flock?
       Where is he who put within him
          his holy spirit,
12   who made his glorious power march
          at the right hand of Moses,
       dividing the waters before them,
       to win for himself an everlasting name,
13   causing them to go through the depths
          sure-footed as horses in the wilderness,
14   like cattle moving down into a valley without
                   stumbling,
          guided*[e]* by the spirit of the LORD?
       So didst thou lead thy people
       to win thyself a glorious name.

15   Look down from heaven and behold
       from the heights where thou dwellest holy and glorious.
          Where is thy zeal, thy valour,
          thy burning and tender love?
16   Stand not aloof;*[f]* for thou art our father,

[a] *That is* Moses *whose name resembles the Heb. verb meaning* draw out,
cp. Exod. 2: 10 and the note there.
[b] and...people: *or, with some MSS.,* and Moses his servant.
[c] *Lit.* from the sea.
[d] *Or* shepherds.
[e] guided: *so Sept.; Heb.* given rest.
[f] Stand not aloof: *prob. rdg.; Heb. obscure in context.*

though Abraham does not know us nor Israel acknow-
    ledge us.
Thou, LORD, art our father;
    thy name is our Ransomer*a* from of old.
Why, LORD, dost thou let us wander from thy ways   17
    and harden our hearts until we cease to fear thee?
    turn again for the sake of thy servants,
        the tribes of thy patrimony.
Why have wicked men trodden down thy   18
    sanctuary,*b*
    why have our enemies trampled on thy shrine?
We have long been reckoned as beyond thy sway,   19
    as if we had not been named thy own.

✻ Verses 7–14 are a hymn-like confession of faith.

7. Like so many psalms, and especially those which describe
conditions of distress, this prayer begins with a recollection of
God's *acts of unfailing love*. The word *ḥesed* – here in the plural
referring to God's *many acts* – begins and ends verse 7; it is
the great covenant word. It is that in God which led to the
formal making of the covenant. *recount* (cp. 62: 6 and comment
on 'you who invoke'): literally here the word is 'I will
make remembrance', apparently before God as well as before
Israel. It is implied in remembering that appropriate action
will inevitably follow.

8–9. This theme leads to the reflection in verses 8f.,
beginning with the recall of the covenant relationship (*my
people* and *my sons*); cp. Exod. 3: 7; 4: 23. But the additional
words *who will not play me false* (verse 8) prepare the mind for
the horrifying words of verse 10. *Surely* (verse 8) represents a
strong Hebrew word suggesting 'contrary to all normal

[*a*] *Or* our Kinsman.
[*b*] Why...sanctuary: *prob. rdg.; Heb.* For a little while they possessed
thy holy people.

expectations'. The translation of verse 9 is based on the Septuagint. The reading of the Authorized Version and the Revised Standard Version is possible but the N.E.B. requires only a different vowel in 'he was afflicted' to produce the word *envoy*. What is referred to is described in Exod. 23: 20 etc. Verse 9 recalls that God *himself* has been Israel's saviour from the exodus and ever since. *love and pity* are both more strongly emotional words than 'love' in verse 7.

10. *his holy spirit:* cp. verse 11 and Ps. 51: 11. These are the only places in the Old Testament where this phrase is used. It would be a mistake to read into the phrase the fuller Christian meaning of the New Testament, and the N.E.B. is right to avoid capital letters. Basically it is an emphatic expression for 'him', as if to draw attention to God's presence and activity. Thus *they* at the beginning of the verse is emphatic in the Hebrew: 'they of all people'.

11–12. *Then men remembered* is a small emendation of the Masoretic Text 'he remembered', which the remainder of the verse requires. The N.E.B. footnote on *drew out* indicates the word-play on the traditional understanding of *Moses*. The ancient versions and earlier English translators appear to have missed the point, and therefore emended the Hebrew. *Where...Where:* God is apparently absent in the present distress of the Jews. Therefore there is the familiar recital of the saving acts of God at the exodus. *Nile:* see the N.E.B. footnote. The equation of the Nile with the sea, as this sentence requires, may be deliberate. Just as in the creation myth God quelled the primeval sea (Ps. 74: 13), so in Israel's history he conquered the Nile. This historical recital largely replaced, in Israel's religion, the Canaanite creation myth, although echoes remain (cp. 51: 9–11).

13. Israel was led securely like cavalry on a firm plain, and contrary to all expectation, through the mighty deep and the fearful wilderness.

14. *guided:* see the N.E.B. footnote. The small emendation, with the support of the Septuagint, may be justified, but

'given rest' with the meaning 'brought into the promised land' (cp. Deut. 12: 9–10) would be a fitting climax.

15–19. **The Lament.** The prayer, in the light of God's mighty work of salvation in the exodus, now turns to the present distress.

15. *Look down...:* cp. Ps. 80: 14. *zeal:* cp. 59: 17 and comment. That God is a zealous (jealous) God forms part of the most ancient recital (Exod. 34: 14). The closing words of this verse express in the strongest possible language Israel's faith in the love of God.

16. *Thou, LORD, art our father:* the statement is not common in the Old Testament, although it occurs in an early psalm, Deut. 32: 6 (cp. Jer. 3: 19; 31: 9; Isa. 64: 8; Mal. 1: 6; 2: 10) yet the concept is deeply embedded in the exodus tradition (Exod. 4: 22f.). The reason for this reluctance to speak of God as father lies in the common understanding, in the world outside Israel, of the god as physically father. Thus Zeus was the father of gods and man. Yet Israel (and the Davidic dynasty) was the son by adoption – i.e. by God's free choice. What is emphasized is not paternity but fatherhood. The same deliberate ambiguity attaches to *Ransomer* (see the N.E.B. footnote *a*). The community after the exile no longer finds comfort in the thought that they are the descendants of Abraham and Israel, to whom the promise of the land was given. Their only hope is in the Father who is the Creator of Israel (64: 8).

17. The question corresponds to the prayer 'Lead us not into temptation.' It is difficult to relate Israel's profound conviction that all events have their origin in God's sovereign will to the equally firm conviction that man is responsible for his wrong-doing. But if the paradox cannot be resolved, it includes the faith that even in man's sinful conduct God is at work for man's salvation. This lies at the heart of the whole biblical faith (cp. Acts 2: 23f.).

18–19. The condition of the land is such that apparently

God is impotent or indifferent; hence the prayer for some
manifest appearing of God in the verses that follow. ✳

64 1^a Why didst thou not rend the heavens and come down,
and make the mountains shudder before thee
2^b as when fire blazes up in brushwood
or fire makes water boil?
then would thy name be known to thy enemies
and nations tremble at thy coming.
3 When thou didst terrible things that we did not look
for,^c
the mountains shuddered before thee.
4 Never has ear heard^d or eye seen
any other god taking the part of those who wait for
him.
5 Thou dost welcome him who rejoices to do what is
right,
who remembers thee in thy ways.
Though thou wast angry, yet we sinned,
in spite of it we have done evil from of old,^e
6 we all become like a man who is unclean
and all our righteous deeds like a filthy rag;^f
we have all withered^g like leaves
and our iniquities sweep us away like the wind.
7 There is no one who invokes thee by name
or rouses himself to cling to thee;

[a] 63: 19b in Heb.
[b] 64: 1 in Heb.
[c] So Sept.; Heb. adds thou hast come down.
[d] Never...heard: prob. rdg.; Heb. They have never heard or listened.
[e] in spite...old: prob. rdg., cp. Sept.; Heb. obscure in context.
[f] Lit. menstrous garment.
[g] have all withered: or are all carried away.

for thou hast hidden thy face from us
   and abandoned*a* us to our iniquities.
But now, LORD, thou art our father;   8
we are the clay, thou the potter,
   and all of us are thy handiwork.
Do not be angry beyond measure, O LORD,   9
and do not remember iniquity for ever;
look on us all, look on thy people.
Thy holy cities are a wilderness,   10
Zion a wilderness, Jerusalem desolate;
   our sanctuary, holy and glorious,   11
   where our fathers praised thee,
   has been burnt to the ground
and all that we cherish is a ruin.
After this, O LORD, wilt thou hold back,   12

   wilt thou keep silence and punish us beyond measure?

✷ 1–7. A prayer for help. This begins with the traditional language of the psalms (cp. Ps. 18: 7), but the divine appearing is to be universally recognized, just as (verse 4) the uniqueness of God is confessed.

   1. *Why* corresponds to a Hebrew exclamation 'O that thou wouldst'.

   3. The coming of God will be, beyond all previous experience or expectation, for judgement and salvation. The words in the footnote may have been an accidental repetition of part of 64: 1, or they may be the response of the congregation deliberately repeating the earlier words.

   4. These words are quoted in a modified form in 1. Cor. 2: 9 in reference to the coming of Jesus.

   5. It is possible that the last word in the Hebrew of verse 4 with a slightly different pronunciation has been omitted by

[*a*] and abandoned: *so Sept.; Heb. unintelligible.*

179

accident from the beginning of this verse, which would then become a prayer 'O that thou wouldst meet....' *remembers* (cp. 63: 7): 'recounts'. *we sinned:* the pronoun introduces a confession of sin which the prophet speaks on behalf of the people.

6. *unclean:* the word means ritually unfit to enter the sanctuary, but is now related to moral and spiritual unfitness which separates from God. This is continued in the words *filthy rag* (literally 'menstruous cloth'). It is not a theological statement, but a statement of fact. The present condition of Israel indicates that God is not with them in spite of their righteous deeds; they are distressed and humiliated and so apparently forsaken by God. The prophet knows that this is not the case and so leads into a prayer for forgiveness and reconciliation.

8–12. The final prayer and appeal to God.

8. The transitional *But now* is an emphatic and direct appeal to God, who may seem to have forsaken his people but is *our father* (cp. 63: 16), who will never abandon what he has created; cp. Jer. 18: 5–6.

9. Cp. Ps. 79: 8. There is no attempt to condone the *iniquity* which has resulted in the present suffering, but there is also the certainty that God will welcome the returning prodigal, as indeed Ps. 79 suggests.

10–11 describe the condition of *Jerusalem* and its *sanctuary* after the Babylonian invasion.

12. The final question expresses not only the distress of the community, but also the faith that God will hear and answer.✶

ORACLES OF JUDGEMENT AND SALVATION

✶ There is a similarity in content within chs. 65 and 66, and even in their structure, which would be more apparent if they were presented in parallel columns. It is evident that within the situation after the exile there is a division between the loyal and the disloyal (cp. 56: 9 – 57: 13), and a recrudes-

cence of pagan practices. Thus there is an alternation of promise and threat, and much in these chapters points to the dawn
of the divine intervention in history which will mark the New
Age in which the evils and limitations of man's present life
will be done away. The judgement of God will extend to all
mankind, as will also the salvation. Artistically and religiously
these chapters form a fitting climax to the book of Isaiah. How
far the contents were originally a unity, or a collection of
various oracles gathered together by a compiler (probably a
member of the Isaianic community), can hardly be determined
with certainty. The passage 65: 1–7 is distinct from the rest
of the chapter; ch. 66 may more probably be regarded as a
collection of distinct oracles. ✶

THE DOOM OF THE DISLOYAL

I was there to be sought by a people who did not ask, **65**
   to be found by men who did not seek me.
I said, 'Here am I, here am I',
   to a nation that did not invoke me by name.
I spread out my hands all day   2
   appealing to an unruly people
who went their evil way,
   following their own devices,
a people who provoked me   3
   continually to my face,
offering sacrifice in gardens, burning incense on brick
      altars,
crouching among graves, keeping vigil all night long, 4
eating swine's flesh, their cauldrons full of a tainted
      brew.
'Stay where you are,' they cry,   5
'do not dare touch me; for I am too sacred for you.'

>   Such people are a smouldering fire,
>   smoking in my nostrils all day long.
> 6   All is on record before me; I will not keep silence;
> 7   I will repay[a] your iniquities,
>   yours and your fathers', all at once, says the LORD,
>   because they burnt incense[b] on the mountains
>   and defied me on the hills;
>   I will first measure out their reward
>   and then pay them in full.

✶ In its context this was intended to be the divine answer to the prayer of 64: 8–12, but the reference to pagan rites in verses 3–5 does not correspond to the sins of ch. 64. They seem to refer more closely to 57: 5–13. The opening words, however, are certainly appropriate to what precedes, and this may account for the present position of these verses. This section is directed to those who, however much they may claim to be Yahweh's people, have shown by their unholy cultic practices that they are rebellious; they have rejected God's gracious invitation, and he will now pronounce judgement against them. Evidently among those who were living in and around Jerusalem there was one section which had abandoned the purity of worship required by the Law. About a century later we have evidence of a corrupted religion in a Jewish colony at Elephantine (cp. *Understanding the Old Testament* in this series, p. 88).

3f. The precise significance of the practices referred to in these verses is obscure, except that they refer to nature cults (verse 3) and necromancy (verse 4). *eating swine's flesh* is a flagrant violation of Deut. 14: 7. It appears that some Jews in their despair were looking for help from pagan deities.

5 reflects an ancient conception of holiness as dangerous and

[a] *Prob. rdg., transposing* and then pay *to follow* reward.
[b] *Or* sacrifices.

contagious; cp. Ezek. 44: 19. Those who engage in such cults are not like the sacrificial smoke that is pleasing to God (Gen. 8: 21) but a stench that provokes wrath.

6–7. The verdict is solemnly *on record*. God will indeed not *keep silence* (64: 12), but now it will be for penal judgement against the apostates.   ✶

SALVATION FOR THE FAITHFUL, DESTRUCTION
FOR THE DISLOYAL

These are the words of the Lord: 8
As there is new wine in a cluster of grapes
and men say, 'Do not destroy it; there is a blessing in it',
 so will I do for my servants' sake:
 I will not destroy the whole nation.
 I will give Jacob children to come after him   9
 and Judah heirs who shall possess my mountains;
  my chosen shall inherit them
 and my servants shall live there.
 Flocks shall range over Sharon,   10
  and the Vale of Achor be a pasture for cattle;
  they shall belong to my people who seek me.
But you that forsake the Lord and forget my holy   11
   mountain,
  who spread a table for the god of Fate,
  and fill bowls of spiced wine in honour of Fortune,
  I will deliver you to your fate, to execution,   12
  and you shall all bend the neck to the sword,
   because I called and you did not answer,
   I spoke and you did not listen;
  and you did what was wrong in my eyes
  and you chose what was against my will.

13   Therefore these are the words of the Lord GOD:
       My servants shall eat but you shall starve;
       my servants shall drink but you shall go thirsty;
       my servants shall rejoice but you shall be put to shame;
14   my servants shall shout in triumph
         in the gladness of their hearts,
       but you shall cry from sorrow
         and wail from anguish of spirit;
15   your name shall be used as an oath by my chosen,
         and the Lord GOD shall give you over to death;
       but his servants he shall call by another name.
16   He who invokes a blessing on himself in the land
       shall do so by the God whose name is Amen,
       and he who utters an oath in the land
       shall do so by the God of Amen;
       the former troubles are forgotten
       and they are hidden from my sight.

✻ This section may be seen as a development of verses 1–7, and leading to a more distinctly eschatological development in verses 17–25. The division in society after the exile is clearly marked; on the one hand are 'my servants' (seven times in this section) and on the other 'you that forsake the LORD'. The words are directly addressed to the apostates, and are introduced by the solemn words of the prophet–messenger. It is possible that we should recognize two prophecies, verses 8–12 and verses 13–16, but the contrast between promise and threat is continued throughout. The important point is made that the real descendants of Jacob and Judah are not primarily those who claim physical descent, but those who are the loyal servants of God (verse 9). Just as the prophet had declared that the people of God would include many who were not of the Israelite nation (56: 6–7), so now he declares that the future of Israel will be fulfilled by a remnant in the Jewish nation. Yet there seems to be a hint (verse 8), if no more, that by this very process of discrimination, all Israel may be saved. For this section was explicitly addressed to the disloyal in order that they might repent and find their true home again in the Israel of God. The argument resembles that of Paul in Rom. 9–11.

8. The opening words would have a familiar sound for those who began the grape harvest. As they gathered the bundles of grapes they might well find some that were imperfect. This was a common experience, and no vine-dresser would destroy the whole harvest or even a whole bunch on that account. In fact there seems to have been a popular song warning against indiscriminate action. (It appears to have provided the melody for Pss. 57–9 and 75 as the titles 'Do not destroy' in the Revised Standard Version suggest.) The mysterious power, *a blessing*, which produces the harvest on the vines, is present in each grape-cluster. Just so, the mysterious power that has preserved Israel through the centuries, the divine blessing, is in this people, and effective unless it is finally rejected. So the condemnation is uttered with the intention of summoning to repentance and salvation. A similar point is made in Matt. 13: 24–30, 47–8.

9. The ancient promise of Gen. 28: 13 is recalled: Israel will again inhabit the land.

10. Moreover the swampy area of Sharon to the north and the barren territory of Achor near the Dead Sea will become fertile pastures.

11. Only those who have rejected the Lord for the pagan deities Fate (Meni) and Fortune (Gad) will have no part in the blessing.

12. *I will deliver:* literally 'I will count, destine' – a word play on Meni (*fate*) in Hebrew. We might paraphrase 'You who trust in Fate will go to your fate.' They have chosen the shadow instead of the substance.

Verses 13–15 express this separation in terms that

recall the blessing and the curse associated with the covenant.

13–14. In the Hebrew each clause has an exclamation preceding *my servants*, emphasizing the solemnity of the sentence pronounced and the contrast between the fate of *my servants* and *you* (the apostates). One may recall the contrast in Matt. 25: 31–46.

15 reverses the ancient blessing to the Patriarchs (Gen. 12: 2 etc.). In a curse, the normal formula would be 'May you become like so-and-so'; cp. Zech. 8: 13. Here it refers back to the judgement on the apostates.

16 is apparently the opposite of verse 15 and refers to 'my servants'. The precise meaning and even translation is not quite clear; the *God whose name is Amen* and the *God of Amen* are identical in Hebrew. *Amen* is a strong affirmation associated with a promise or statement and is so used by Jesus in the Gospels; cp. Mark 3: 28, 'I tell you this', and John 1: 51, 'In truth...' It may be that *Amen* is the new name for 'my servants'. They are the faithful, and their God alone will be the assurance of the blessing. This is an essential element in the New Age in which *former troubles* will no longer be present. This introduces the next section. ✳

A WORLD TRANSFORMED

17   For behold, I create
new heavens and a new earth.
Former things shall no more be remembered
nor shall they be called to mind.

18   Rejoice and be filled with delight,
you boundless realms which I create;
for I create Jerusalem to be a delight
and her people a joy;

19 I will take delight in Jerusalem and rejoice in my
people;

    weeping and cries for help
  shall never again be heard in her.
There no child shall ever again die an infant,   20
  no old man fail to live out his life;
    every boy shall live his hundred years before he dies,
whoever falls short of a hundred shall be despised.[a]
Men shall build houses and live to inhabit them,   21
plant vineyards and eat their fruit;
    they shall not build for others to inhabit   22
  nor plant for others to eat.
My people shall live the long life of a tree,
and my chosen shall enjoy the fruit of their labour.
They shall not toil in vain or raise children for 23
      misfortune.
  For they are the offspring of the blessed of the LORD
      and their issue after them;
before they call to me, I will answer,   24
and while they are still speaking I will listen.
The wolf and the lamb shall feed together   25
and the lion shall eat straw like cattle.[b]
They shall not hurt or destroy in all my holy mountain,
      says the LORD.

* It is characteristic of Old Testament prophecy when it
points to the New Age that it is not other-worldly, but sees
this world transformed or restored to its original purpose in
God's creation of it.

   17. The *new heavens and a new earth* are this physical world
in which men will be free from the hardships of life.

   18–19. Jerusalem will become in very truth 'the city of

    [a] Or cursed.
    [b] *Prob. rdg.; Heb. adds* and the food of the snake shall be dust.

God' (Ps. 46) and 'the joy of the whole earth' (Ps. 48: 2), the centre of true worship in which God himself *will take delight*, as Israel in its highest acts of worship knew that it should be.

20. Nature itself will respond to the divine will to which his people are loyal. It is a new, or renewed, creation. His people will know abundant life. The span of life will be a *hundred years*, and if a man fails to reach that age it will be a sign of divine displeasure.

21–2. Life will be secure and free from the threat of invasion (cp. 62: 8–9).

24–5. The restoration of the Davidic monarchy is not mentioned, but the fulfilment of all the hopes of Israel centred on that monarchy is specifically referred to in verse 25, a quotation from 11: 6–9. There is no need for God's representative, the king, when God himself is at all times present (verse 24).

There are many echoes of this passage in the New Testament (cp. Rom. 8: 21). The remarkable feature of this vision is not simply its beauty and splendour, but that it was spoken by one who experienced the limitations of life in the early age after the exile, yet knew with great certainty the victory of God's purpose for man. ✶

FINAL BLESSINGS AND CURSES

✶ While in this closing chapter of the book there are many difficulties of interpretation and even of translation in individual verses, the main themes are clear enough. There have arisen in the community after the exile serious divisions, largely brought about by differences of a cultic nature. The words are aimed to support and encourage those who revere the word of the LORD. In spite of their suffering at the hands of their fellow Jews, they can be assured that the LORD is about to come with judgement on those who have been seduced by pagan practices, and with salvation for those who in simple piety seek to do his will. Indeed they will see the day when there will be a great ingathering of the nations who will not only bring back Jews who have been dispersed among the nations, but the Gentiles themselves will acknowledge the God of Israel and become fully integrated into the Jewish community. Perhaps one of the most remarkable features of this chapter is the contrast between the universalistic spirit displayed towards the Gentiles, for so long the oppressors of the Jews, and the vigorous condemnation of those in Judaism who are disloyal to their ancient faith. Considering the external circumstances of the age after the exile this universalism is little short of miraculous.

The difficulties of interpretation arise partly from our paucity of knowledge about the precise historical situation in which these oracles were uttered, as well as of the religious practices referred to. There is room for difference of opinion, but the view taken in the following comments is that they belong to the early period after the exile, after the work of Haggai and Zechariah but before that of Nehemiah.

One cause of tension was immediately apparent. The majority of the Jews in and around Jerusalem were the descendants of those who had remained behind when the Jews deported by the Babylonians were in exile. They had continued in the religious practices of the deuteronomic reform, however much debased during the reigns of the kings who followed Josiah. It is unlikely that they would see themselves as Jeremiah's 'bad figs' (Jer. 24: 8–10)! On the other hand there were those who had returned from exile after the decree of Cyrus, whose religious outlook was more akin to that of Ezekiel and Lev. 17–26, though doubtless influenced by the noble vision of Second Isaiah. But the divisions were not as clear-cut as that might suggest. Undoubtedly disillusionment had affected those who returned. Yet the rebuilding of the temple had restored some of their hopes, and may well have attracted to them some of the others. But pagan practices almost inevitably affected both groups, especially when the rebuilding of the temple was followed by none of the expectations

associated with Zechariah's oracles. We have suggested that
Isa. 65 reflects this situation. There are features of Isa. 66 that
resemble what is found in Isa. 65. It is probable that Isa. 66 is a
collection of oracles or fragments of oracles from this same
period, although it is not always easy to see how they should
be divided. We may follow in the main the divisions suggested by the N.E.B. while recognizing that other divisions are
possible. ✲

TRUE WORSHIP AND FALSE

66   These are the words of the LORD:
        Heaven is my throne and earth my footstool.
        Where will you build a house for me,
            where shall my resting-place be?
2   All these are of my own making
        and all these are mine.*a*
            This is the very word of the LORD.

        The man I look to is a man down-trodden and
            distressed,
            one who reveres my words.
3   But to sacrifice an ox or to*b* kill a man,
        slaughter a sheep or break a dog's neck,
        offer grain or offer pigs' blood,
        burn incense as a token and worship an idol –
        all these are the chosen practices of men
            who*c* revel in their own loathsome rites.
4   I too will practise those wanton rites of theirs
            and bring down on them the very things they dread;

[a] mine: *so Sept.; Heb. om.*
[b] to sacrifice an ox or to: *or those who sacrifice an ox and...*
[c] are the chosen practices of men who: *or have chosen their own
devices and...*

for I called and no one answered,
  I spoke and no one listened.
They did what was wrong in my eyes
  and chose practices not to my liking.

* Verses 1-2 may be taken as one oracle, although the N.E.B.
associates the closing words with verse 3. There is an obvious
reference to 2 Sam. 7: 4-7 and 1 Kings 8: 27-30. The words
have been seen as a criticism of Haggai, or a word of consola-
tion to the returned exiles whose hopes for rebuilding the
temple immediately on their return were frustrated. But they
could well be spoken after the temple had been rebuilt in
order to check the wrong kind of dependence on the sanctuary
(cp. Jer. 7: 4). Solomon's prayer likewise followed the building of his temple. It is true to the spirit of the Old Testament
teaching of priest, prophet and psalmist that God is independent of any *house* or *resting-place* that man may construct; but
such a house may well be a focal point for man's worship of
God. It still remains true that temple or no temple, God
looks first for genuine humility and reverence.

3-4 should be taken as an independent oracle. The language
in the Hebrew is much condensed, and in this respect it
resembles the language of the book of Proverbs. Translation is
difficult since in English one has to provide the link-words:
the Revised Standard Version, 'is like'; the N.E.B., *or*; the
Jerusalem Bible, 'some...some'. It is unlikely that the prophet
is condemning all outward forms of worship, but rather the
mingling of pagan rites with true Jewish worship. It is known
that human sacrifice and eating of *dog's* flesh was an aspect of
Phoenician worship, and contact with swine was forbidden
on religious grounds in Judaism. Earlier prophets had con-
demned the sacrifices and prayers of those who neglected
God's requirements of justice (Isa. 1: 10-27; Mic. 6: 6-8).
This prophet may be understood to say that those who
worship pagan deities cannot truly worship Yahweh. The

Jews must choose; God also makes his choice (the N.E.B. *practise* in verse 4 corresponds to the same verb as *chosen* in verse 3, and to *I...will practise* and *chose practices* in verse 4). The *loathsome rites* they have adopted will become the means of their destruction. It is, indeed, historically true that the distinctiveness of Jewish religion preserved the Jews as a community through the following centuries. The closing words of verse 4 repeat those in 65: 12. *

THE FATE OF THE DISLOYAL

5 Hear the word of the LORD, you who revere his word:
      Your fellow-countrymen who hate you,
         who spurn you because you bear my name, have said,
      'Let the LORD show his glory,
      then we shall see you rejoice';
      but they shall be put to shame.
6 That roar from the city, that uproar in the temple,
      is the sound of the LORD dealing retribution to his foes.

* 5 seems to be an independent oracle distinguishing the pious, *you who revere his word*, from unfaithful fellow-Jews. *fellow-countrymen*: literally brothers, i.e. co-religionists. The same word is used in the New Testament in the speeches of Peter (Acts 2: 29 – N.E.B. 'my friends' – of fellow-Jews) and by Paul (1 Cor. 1: 1 – N.E.B. 'colleague' – of a fellow Christian). There were divisions in the society but no schism. There is no suggestion of the tragic break that later occurred in the fourth century between Jews and Samaritans. (There is no evidence of a Samaritan community in this period.) The mocking tone in the speech of the opponents recalls 5: 19.

6. Another fragment, apparently referring to the Day of the LORD, a day of judgement on the nations; cp. Joel 3: 16. Clearly the temple has been rebuilt. *

THE RENEWAL OF GOD'S PEOPLE

Shall a woman bear a child without pains?   7
give birth to a son before the onset of labour?
   Who has heard of anything like this?   8
   Who has seen any such thing?
Shall a country be born after one day's labour,
shall a nation be brought to birth all in a moment?
But Zion, at the onset of her pangs, bore her sons.
   Shall I bring to the point of birth and not deliver?   9
      the LORD says;
   shall I who deliver close the womb?
      your God has spoken.

Rejoice with Jerusalem and exult in her,   10
      all you who love her;
   share her joy with all your heart,
   all you who mourn over her.
Then you may suck and be fed from the breasts that   11
      give comfort,
delighting in her plentiful milk.
   For thus says the LORD: 12
I will send peace flowing over her like a river,
and the wealth of nations like a stream in flood;
     it shall suckle you,
      and you shall be carried in their arms
      and dandled on their knees.
   As a mother comforts her son,   13
   so will I myself comfort you,
      and you shall find comfort in Jerusalem.
   This you shall see and be glad at heart,   14

your limbs shall be as fresh as grass in spring;
the LORD shall make his power known among his
servants
and his indignation felt among his foes.

15   For see, the LORD is coming in fire,
with his chariots like a whirlwind,
to strike home with his furious anger
and with the flaming fire of his reproof.

16   The LORD will judge by fire,
with fire he will test all living men,
and many will be slain by the LORD;

17   those who hallow and purify themselves in garden-
rites,
one*a* after another in a magic ring,
those who eat the flesh of pigs and rats*b* and all vile
vermin,
shall meet their end, one and all,
says the LORD,

18*a*   for I know*c* their deeds and their thoughts.

✷ 7–9 describe the miraculous rebirth of Jerusalem, which up
to Nehemiah's day must have seemed impossible. It is
emphasized that this will be by a swift and unexpected act of
God.

10–14. The New Jerusalem is the source of all joy and the
total welfare of *all you who love her.* One can imagine that this
was a prophetic song for those who loyally, yet wistfully,
sang the Songs of Zion, Pss. 46; 48; 122. She is described as
the mother of the people of God, and therefore the earthly
counterpart of God who in a remarkable phrase is also likened
to a mother lovingly comforting her children (verse 13).

[a] one: *so Pesh.; Heb. om.* [b] *Or* jerboas.
[c] know: *so Pesh.; Heb. om.*

15–16. This is another oracle of universal judgement, apparently included here because of the closing words of verse 14. The language is similar to some of the Psalms, e.g. 50: 3, and may be seen as an answer to the pleading in Isa. 64: 1–3. The fragment in verse 6 may have been part of this oracle.

17–18*a* is again a fragment of an oracle and not a continuation of verse 16. It appears to belong to 65: 3–5. *in a magic ring* is some kind of rite similar to that in Ezek. 8: 11. The significance is quite obscure to us, but possibly some relic of it is preserved in present-day children's games where they 'follow the leader' in a winding movement.

UNIVERSAL SALVATION AND JUDGEMENT

Then I myself[a] will come to gather all nations and   18*b*
  races,
  and they shall come and see my glory;
  and I will perform a sign among them.   19
I will spare some of them and send them to the nations,
  to Tarshish, Put,[b] and Lud,[c]
  to Meshek, Rosh,[d] Tubal, and Javan,[e]
distant coasts and islands which have never yet heard
    of me
  and have not seen my glory;
  these shall announce that glory among the nations.
From every nation they shall bring your countrymen   20
  on horses, in chariots and wagons,
    on mules and dromedaries,

[a] I myself: *so Sept.; Heb.* it.
[b] *So Sept.; Heb. unintelligible.*
[c] *Or* Lydia.
[d] Meshek, Rosh: *prob. rdg.; Heb.* those who draw the bow.
[e] *Or* Greece.

> as an offering to the LORD,
>   on my holy mountain Jerusalem,
>   says the LORD,
>   as the Israelites bring offerings
>   in pure vessels to the LORD's house;
> 21 and some of them I will take for priests, for[a] Levites,
>   says the LORD.
> 22 For, as the new heavens and the new earth
>   which I am making shall endure in my sight,
>   says the LORD,
>   so shall your race and your name endure;
> 23   and month by month at the new moon,
>   week by week on the sabbath,
>   all mankind shall come to bow down before me,
>   says the LORD;
> 24   and they shall come out and see
>   the dead bodies of those who have rebelled against me;
>   their worm shall not die nor their fire be quenched,
>   and they shall be abhorred by all mankind.

✻ 18*b*–21. Although these verses form a magnificent introduction to what follows, they may best be treated independently. They contain echoes of earlier prophecy (49: 22; 62: 10). They go far beyond them in their universalistic hope and evangelistic expectation. Not only will all nations share in Israel's supreme privilege of seeing the manifestation of Yahweh's sovereignty (perhaps in the temple), but those whom God *will spare* (apparently in the day of judgement) will then go as missionaries all over the world to proclaim the glory of God! The place-names are meant to indicate all the ends of the earth. *Tarshish:* a Phoenician

[a] Or, *with Sept.,* and.

colony in Spain. *Put* and *Lud*: in Africa. *Meshek, Rosh, Tubal* are peoples on the shores of the Black Sea. *Javan*: Greece or the Ionians of Asia Minor. But they are all referred to as the far-off peoples of the world, the *distant coasts and islands.* These are to escort exiled Jews back to Jerusalem in great splendour as their grain-*offering to the LORD*. Then comes the incredible climax to the prophecy. From their number, some of the Gentiles will be divinely appointed as levitical priests! This is in very truth a new heaven and a new earth.

22–3. This section speaks of the continuance of the Jewish people into the New Age, assured by their worship. Here, too, the vision of Jew and Gentile united in the worship of God and the celebration of the sacramental acts is part of the vision. It would be pedantic to argue that they could not all flock to Jerusalem. The holy city has become the symbolic centre for those who worship the one true God 'in spirit and in truth'. What is required in the Law of the Jew (Num. 28: 10, 14) is to be fulfilled by *all mankind*. The same vision, connected with Israel's greatest festival, the Feast of Taber-nacles, is found also in Zech. 14: 16. That book also continues into a declaration of universal judgement (Isa. 66: 24; cp. Zech. 14: 17–19), although this is not the final word in Zechariah.

24 describes the final doom upon *those who have rebelled against me*. This can only refer to the unfaithful in Israel of whom the prophet speaks in these last two chapters. That means that combined with the universalism of verses 22–3 we have the severest judgement on those who have proved unworthy of the great revelation entrusted to them, the apostate Jews. Apparently the *dead bodies* will be in the Valley of Hinnom (Ge-Hinnom, Gehenna) at the foot of Mt Zion (cp. Jer. 7: 31–3). This was in the days before the exile a place where a pagan god was worshipped, and later became an appropriate term for the modern English 'Hell'. This is the origin of the terminology in the New Testament; cp. Mark 9: 47f. That the book of Isaiah, and especially

chs. 40–66, should end on such a note seems to us both aesthetically and religiously inappropriate. We may say that it represents the mind of one who took with great seriousness Israel's privilege in being God's means and agent of his self-revelation to all mankind. A similar attitude appears in Heb. 12: 22–9. Nevertheless we can only assent to the instruction of the Jewish rabbis that verse 24 should be followed by a repetition of verse 23. This is still the practice in the synagogue. ✻

✻   ✻   ✻   ✻   ✻   ✻   ✻   ✻   ✻   ✻   ✻   ✻   ✻   ✻   ✻

THE TEACHING OF ISAIAH 56–66

We have seen that it is difficult to find a sequence of thought, or indeed consistency of presentation, within these chapters. In part this is due to our ignorance of the details of the history after the year 538 B.C. The brief reference in Ezra 1–6 and the picture presented in Haggai, Zechariah 1–8 and Malachi make it clear that it was a period of alternating hope and disappointment. Certainly the conditions were far removed from those envisaged in Isa. 40–55. Some Jews returned, but only a minority. Whatever hopes they may have had were quickly frustrated by the impoverished conditions they met, and it appears that neither they nor their plans were welcomed by those who had continued to live in a much restricted territory, whose energies were almost exhausted by their efforts to gain a bare subsistence from the soil. If, as seems likely, we have the words of more than one prophet, they were undoubtedly seeking to relate the great words of their master (Isa. 40–55) to the situation they met. The message of the prophet of the exile remains in these chapters, but it is directed to those who live in Judaea. It is basically the same, but the existing circumstances demand different applications and forms of expression. Sometimes we find a repetition of the message of comfort (57: 15–19; 61: 1), sometimes a return to judgement reminiscent of the eighth-century prophets (57:

1–13). Here too is the hope of the restoration of Zion (62: 1–12) but the reference to sabbath observance and sacrifice in 56: 2; 58: 13–14 is new. Once more there is the great hope of the conversion of the nations (66: 18–19), but also a terrifying judgement on the nations (63: 1–6).

In summarizing the teaching of these chapters it is particularly important to recognize those who are addressed, whether or not the prophecies are from one or more speakers. (1) There were those who returned from Babylon inspired by the words of Second Isaiah and of Ezekiel. (2) There were those who had remained in a territorially much reduced and impoverished land, whose experience is reflected in Lamentations, and whose 'Law', even if honoured mainly in the breach, was Deuteronomy. Many of these had lapsed into old Canaanite religious practices. (3) There were those, not actually addressed, who surrounded this much reduced country, and formed a continual threat to its life and integrity.

If, once again, we begin with the work of salvation it is in these chapters related to a very different situation. Once more the hearers are summoned to prepare for deliverance (56: 1) but the preparation will consist in fulfilling the moral and ritual requirements of the Law. Elsewhere it appears that the hearers have been disappointed, but we are told that what prevents their realization of God's salvation is their own evil-doing (59: 1–8). But salvation is related not to a release from conditions of exile; it is related to poverty, the restoration of devastated Jerusalem (62: 8–12) and enemy hostility (60: 18). Salvation is much more closely connected with the conditions of the New Age (60: 16; 61: 10). It is remarkable that the universalism of Second Isaiah appears to be present to a greater extent in these chapters (60: 1–16; 61: 5–9; 66: 18b–23), although there is greater emphasis on the subordination of the Gentiles. This is simply to say that the prophet's word was addressed to a real situation; the vision of the prophet of the exile had to be related to circumstances that superficially denied that vision. It may well be that the addition of these chapters made it, humanly speaking, possible for Isa. 40–55 to be preserved as the hope of Israel, when that hope was in danger of immediate frustration. God is still the Saviour but his work of salvation is less from external foes than that of delivering his ransomed people from the moral and religious evils that threaten to corrupt the Jewish community. His salvation extends to the whole world of mankind, and so does his judgement. But if his work of salvation is world-embracing, his severest words of judgement are spoken to those who claim to be his people. It is fundamentally the same thinking that occurs in Rom. 11, and indeed Paul quotes from Isa. 65: 1–2 in Rom. 10: 20–1.

A NOTE ON FURTHER READING

A fuller commentary on this part of the book of Isaiah may be found in C. Westermann, *Isaiah 40–66* (S.C.M. Old Testament Library, 1969) and C. R. North, *The Second Isaiah* [Isa. 40–55] (O.U.P., 1964).

Probably the most inclusive discussion on the servant poems in English may be found in C. R. North, *The Suffering Servant in Deutero-Isaiah* (O.U.P., 1956). E. J. Kissane, *Isaiah 40–66* (Dublin, 1943) presupposes a knowledge of the Hebrew text.

Other commentaries that will be found useful are: C. R. North, *Isaiah 40–55* (S.C.M. Torch Bible Commentaries, 1952); D. R. Jones, *Isaiah 56–66* and *Joel* (S.C.M. Torch Commentaries, 1964); J. M. McKenzie, *Second Isaiah*, Anchor Bible (Doubleday and Co., 1968); J. Muilenberg, *Isaiah 40–66*, Interpreter's Bible, Vol. 5 (Nelson, 1956).

Although only selected chapters are discussed, the volume by P. R. Ackroyd, *Israel under Babylon and Persia*, New Clarendon Bible (O.U.P., 1970), should be consulted.

A valuable book for background information on the history and religious developments of the period is P. R. Ackroyd, *Exile and Restoration*, Old Testament Library (S.C.M., 1968). J. B. Pritchard (ed.), *Ancient Near Eastern Texts Relating to the Old Testament*, 3rd edition (Princeton U.P., 1969) and D. Winton Thomas (ed.), *Documents from Old Testament Times* (Oliver and Boyd, Harper and Row, 1961) both contain the texts of contemporary documents.

INDEX

INDEX

Palestine 2, 6, 13, 85, 101

peace 30, 84, 85, 126, 137, 141, 151, 159

Persia 38, 126

Persian Empire 7, 168

prayer 4, 75, 172f., 175–8

predict, prediction 37–9

priest(s) 12f., 41, 114, 164, 197

prophet(s) 2–4, 6, 8f., 11f., 17

Psalms and Second Isaiah 3, 106, 172; contacts of language and style 48, 71, 96, 110, 140, 170, 172

Put 197

Rahab 100

ransomed 169, 200

Ransomer (Redeemer) 12, 34, 49, 60, 126, 131, 177

reconciliation 12, 109

religion: Canaanite (Phoenician) 136, 167, 176, 191; at Elephantine 182; Jewish (Israelite) 6, 61, 176, 191f.; Persian 30; *see also* Babylon

'remember', meaning of 75, 176, 180

righteousness of God 42, 48, 66, 68, 71, 84, 100, 131, 133, 145f., 152, 163f.

Ruler of history 4, 23, 84, 128

sabbath(s) 144, 147, 199

sacrifice(s) 55, 114, 182f., 191

salvation 35, 49, 56, 70, 88f., 109, 125–30, 199, 200

Samaritans 192

Saviour 22f., 126–8, 176, 200

Scroll(s), Dead Sea 1, 19, 38, 39, 62, 68, 114, 119

sea 45, 100f.

Sela 45

Servant: function 40, 42, 88f., 95f., 109, 129; identity 10–14, 40, 89, 108, 129; *see also* Israel

Servant Poems 9–14, 42, 88, 95f., 108–15, 129, 161f., authorship 2, 9f.

shalom see peace

Sheol 71

shepherd 21, 64, 65, 134

Sheshbazzar 153

sign 139

spirit: as divine power 40f., 57, 84, 118; of God (Yahweh) 23, 126, 162, 176; as wind 34

'sprinkle', meaning of 111

suffering 10–12, 108–13, 170

Syene 90

Tarshish 196f.

temple of Jerusalem: destroyed 5, 92; rebuilt 2, 7, 133, 153, 157, 168, 172, 189, 192; heavenly 157

torah 41, 48

truth (faithfulness) 152, 186

vengeance 78, 163, 172; *see also* vindication

victory 30, 71, 114, 123, 129; *see also* righteousness of God

vindication 78, 103, 110, 119, 167

widow 79, 103

wife 117, 126

word of the LORD 4, 20, 72, 125, 150

worship: Canaanite 147; Israelite (Jewish) 4, 6f., 14, 25f., 56, 70, 83, 147, 188, 191, 197; in New Age 8; wrong worship 55, 60f., 182

Yahweh 6f., 22, 26, 37, 42, 52, 70–2, 126–9, 191; *see also* God of Israel

zeal 152, 177

Zechariah 2, 9, 133, 167, 189f., 197, 198

Zerubbabel 153, 157

Zion 3, 85, 93, 106, 158, 167; as Israel 20, 70, 163; restored 1, 85, 99, 159; *see also* Jerusalem

Zoroaster 30